U0693949

ANNUAL REPORT OF THE CHINESE INSURANCE MARKET 2015

2015 中国保险市场年报

The State Council Released Opinions on Accelerating the Development of Modern Insurance Service Industry

Insurance Makes Life Better

As an important industry in modern economy and a primary means of risk management, insurance is a symbol of the development of a society's civilization, economy and social governance capability.

Efforts shall be made to strive to reform and innovate, further open up, strengthen the market, improve the market environment so as to develop a more competitive, innovative and vigorous modern insurance service industry, and make insurance a pillar in a sound financial system, a key protection for better livelihood, a new means of efficient social management, an engine for the improvement of economic quality and economic growth, and a boost for the transformation of government functions.

By 2020, a modern insurance service industry is to be in place to provide comprehensive protection and exert functions needed in economic development and social progress. China, at that time, will have not only a big insurance industry but also a strong one. China's insurance penetration will be 5%, and density will be RMB 3500 Yuan. Insurance will be an effective stabilizer of the society and a booster of the economy.

Photos by staff of the insurance industry

Contents

**Message from the
Chairman of the CIRC**

2014 has been a historic year for the insurance industry. In August, the State Council publicized *Several Opinions on Accelerating the Development of Modern Insurance Service Industry,* putting forward a blueprint for insurance reform, development and regulation in the new situation for the strategic goal of building a world-class insurance industry. Two months later, the State Council issued *Several Opinions on Accelerating the Development of Commercial Health Insurance,* unprecedentedly defining the important role of commercial health insurance in deepening medical and health system reform, developing health service industry and economic upgrading. These two groundbreaking, leaf-turning documents were milestones in the history of the Chinese insurance industry.

During the past year, under the guidance of the CPC Central Committee and the State Council, the insurance industry has made a historic stride forward and is now embracing a future of new development, seeing steady progress in service, regulation, risk control and growth.

Fast Growth of Insurance Business

Despite the economic downturn last year when target GDP growth rate was lowered, painful structural adjustment was going on and the previous stimulus policies had almost been digested, the insurance industry entered the fast track of development through deepening reform and streamlining administration. In terms of business growth, the year 2014 saw national premium income hitting RMB 2 trillion Yuan[1] for the first time, up by 17.5%, which is record high since the outbreak of the international financial crisis. Non-life premium income was RMB 720.35 billion Yuan, up by 16% YoY. Life premium income registered RMB 1.3 trillion Yuan, up by 18.4% YoY. The business mix of the whole industry has been further adjusted, witnessing high growth in products that support the real economy, improve people's well-being and offer protection. To be more specific, we saw 66.1% growth of guarantee insurance, 77.2% growth of annuity insurance and 41.9% of health insurance. The year 2014 was also the most profitable year for the insurance industry. The total profit for insurance companies is RMB 193.42 billion Yuan, up by 91.4% YoY. Insurance asset management yields are RMB 535.88 billion Yuan, up by 46.5% YoY, a record high. Insurance investment return rate is 6.3%, 1.3 percentage points higher than that of 2013 and the highest in the past 5 years.

---

[1] If not otherwise footnoted, all the data in this annual report are based on *Enterprise Accounting Criteria Interpretation No.2.*

Reform and Innovation Continued to Deepen

We believe that comprehensive, deeper reform is the solution for the insurance industry in the adverse situation. We implemented a lot of reforms in the past year. Pricing reform was pressed ahead to give the market the decisive role in resource allocation. The market-based reform plans for pricing of universal insurance and auto insurance have been submitted to the State Council for approval. Market entrance and exit mechanism was further improved. We encouraged innovative players such as insurance captives, mutuals and internet insurers to enter the market. Insurance asset management reform went deeper, diversifying asset allocation and bringing risks under control. Catastrophe insurance made progress. We worked out a plan for the catastrophe insurance mechanism, developed products, established a pool, carried out pilot projects and will deliver groundbreaking outcomes that the public has been looking forward to.

A Bigger Role in Serving Economic Development and Social Progress

To serve economic development and social progress is a mission of the insurance industry. In 2014, we witnessed a greater role of the insurance industry in this area by complementing social security system, participating in social management, providing protection for agriculture, the rural areas and the rural population. The total insured amount in 2014 was RMB 1114 trillion Yuan, 25.5% more than that of 2013. The insurance industry paid RMB 719.44 billion Yuan in compensation and payout, 15.9% more than in 2013. 392 programs of the major illness insurance were launched in 27 provinces to cover 700 million people. Insurers managed medical protection programs covering 320 million people. Agriculture insurance registered premium income of RMB 32.58 billion Yuan (+ 6.3% YoY) and insured amount of RMB 1.6 trillion Yuan (+17.7% YoY). RMB 1.1 trillion Yuan of insurance fund was invested in infrastructure project, up 56.8% from the beginning of the year, among which RMB 107.25 billion Yuan was invested in shantytowns transformation and protection house construction. Export credit insurance achieved premium income of USD 2.7 billion (+8.2% YoY), with the insured amount totaling USD 380.45 billion, contributing significantly to stabilizing export transaction.

Strengthened Risk Control

In the complex situation of 2014, we carried out a series of inspections based on risk assessment results of the key areas. The purpose of these inspections was to strengthen internal control and external supervision, to contain irregularities and illegal practices. By doing so, we saw no regional or systemic risks outbreaks in 2014. These inspections included on-site corporate governance inspection, theme inspection on agricultural insurance, compliance inspection on major illness insurance and a mop-up campaign in insurance intermediaries market. Insurance anti-money laundering mechanism was also established. Anti-fraud and anti-illegal fund raising campaigns were carried out. We paid great attention to risks concerning concentrated maturity payouts, policy surrenders, inadequate solvency, liquidity and asset management. The insurance industry in general was strong in terms of solvency, with RMB 720.7 billion Yuan of solvency surplus. Only 1 insurer did not meet solvency requirements.

Consumer Protection Stepped up

We paid great attention to insurance consumers' biggest concerns. In 2014, we continued to improve claims settlement of auto insurance and punished life insurance misleading selling practices. 7.35 million pending non-life claims were settled. Enforcement was tightened to ensure the authenticity of customer information. Insurers were asked to supervise their agents more stringently. Under the guidance of CIRC, the Insurance Association of China conducted a satisfaction survey on the services of life insurers to call their attention to providing better services. Insurance disputes were handled carefully. The 12378 hotline for complaints received 245,000 calls. 98.5% of those who called expressed satisfaction with the way their complaints were handled. CIRC processed 28,000 complaints in 2014. On top of this, we issued *CIRC's Guiding Opinions on Strengthening Insurance Consumer Protection* and drafted *China Insurance Credit System Construction Plan (2015-2020)*. We also established 6 channels for consumer education, namely, on our official website, in newspaper columns, pamphlets, official micro-blog and official we-chat and in promotion activities.

Regulatory Modernization Going forward Steadily

2014 has been a year of regulatory modernization for CIRC. We did that by taking in the international regulatory reform experience and integrating it with our own realities. The amendments to the *Insurance Law* have been drafted. 4 administrative rules and measures have been revised or issued. 4,798 normative documents have been abolished, cutting down the total number of these documents by almost 80%. China Risk Oriented Solvency System (C-ROSS), a risk-oriented and internationally comparable solvency system that reflects the features of the Chinese insurance market has been completed, including its 17 rules. We engaged more actively in international interaction and cooperation, for example, in the designing and field test of IAIS ComFrame, ICS and in the selection of GSIIs. We worked with the regulators of Hong Kong and Macau in anti-fraud activities and formed a long-term mechanism among the mainland, Chinese Taipei, Hong Kong and Macau to combat fraud.

When we look back on the year 2014, we see that we have cracked some hard nuts and made a series of historic breakthroughs though reform and innovation. We see a stronger insurance industry with a better public image and higher social status, and a bigger voice in international standard setting activities. We find that the insurance industry has become an important player in governance of the country and in the drive for governance modernization. We see that China now has a significant role in the global insurance paradigm. We have achieved these under the leadership of the CPC Central Committee and the State Council, with the support of our brother ministries and local governments, and because all the insurance professionals have worked hard. On behalf of the Party Committee of CIRC, I would like to thank all the people who have contributed or supported our reform and development cause.

The year 2015 will be the last year to complete the *twelfth five-year plan*. It is a critical year for comprehensively deepening reform as well as a beginning year for rule by law and stricter party discipline. The economy bears significance in this year. We must fully implement the spirit of the 18th National Congress of the CPC, and the 3rd and 4th Plenums of the 18th Central Committee of the CPC to advance our work while maintaining stability and to enhance economic development quality and efficiency. In the economic "new normal", we must drive innovation, perfect risk control and keep the growth of the insurance industry reasonably fast. This requires further progress in industry and in regulation. We must bring our work to a higher level so as to make greater contribution to the economic development and social progress of China.

Xiang Junbo
Chairman of the China Insurance Regulatory Commission
June 22, 2015

02

Social Progress and Economic Development

- Steady Growth of Economy-Foundation for the Development of the Insurance Industry
- Public Welfare Improving Continuously, Providing the Insurance Industry with Broader Room for Development
- The Financial System Ran Steadily with Further Improved Capacities in Serving the Economy and Society

2014 has been a challenging year of complexities and difficulties. The global economy was struggling to recover with divergent situations in major economies. At home, the domestic economy faced increasing downside pressure. The Chinese people, under the strong leadership of the CPC Central Committee, addressed the challenges and continued to forge ahead, fulfilling the anticipated full-year goal of the economic and social development of 2014 and making a firm step towards the goal of building a well-off society. The drive for comprehensively deepening reform achieved a good start, rule by law is well on the way and the party discipline has been strengthened.

Steady Growth of Economy-Foundation for the Development of the Insurance Industry

In 2014, the Chinese government led and united all nationalities of this country to understand the "new normal", meet its challenges and try to lead the "new normal" through reform and innovation. Through hard work, the national economy grew steadily with an upgraded economic structure, higher quality of growth and better well-being of the Chinese people.

Stable Growth of the Economy

The year 2014 witnessed stable growth of the economy, which was in a reasonable range. The Chinese economy became more coordinated and sustainable. China's GDP totaled RMB 63.6 trillion Yuan, up by 7.4% YoY. The full year fiscal revenue amounted to RMB 14 trillion Yuan (+8.6% YoY), including RMB 11.9 trillion Yuan of tax revenue (+7.8% YoY). The state foreign exchange reserve reached USD 3.8 trillion, up by USD 21.7 billion from the end of 2013.

Reform and Opening up Going Deeper

In 2014, China saw further deepening of reform. Market vitality was stimulated, effectively offsetting the downside pressure. Key reforms made big progress. Plans for budget management reform and taxation system reform have been set. The floating range for deposit interest rate and exchange rate was expanded. Pilot projects for private banks advanced. The pricing reform concerning energy, transportation, environmental protection and telecommunications has been accelerated. The government continued role-shifting and administrative streamlining. The departments and ministries under the State Council cancelled or delegated to local levels 246 administrative approval items; cancelled 29 competitions and rewards; cancelled 149 professional qualification or recognition requirements; and cut down the investment project catalogue subject to government approval. Business registration system was reformed and 12.93 million market entities were newly registered. The China Pilot Free Trade Zone was expanded from Shanghai to Guangdong, Tianjin and Fujian. The FDI that China received last year totaled USD 119.6 billion. The outbound investment was USD 102.9 billion. China launched free trade zone projects with Iceland and Switzerland. The free trade negotiations with Korea and Australia have basically been completed. International cooperation in railway, electric power, oil and gas and telecommunications achieved important outcomes.

Structural Adjustment Stepped up

In 2014, when problems with the economic structure became prominent, the Chinese government conducted a differentiated industry policy to optimize the industrial structure and foster new growth engines such as the service sector. More specifically, rising strategic industries such as mobile internet, integrated circuit, high-end equipment manufacturing and new energy automobiles were encouraged. Internet finance became the most eye-catching new industry. E-commerce, logistics and express delivery grew fast. Cultural and creative industry boomed. Meanwhile, 15 key industries with excessive production capacity including steel, iron, and cement abandoned inefficient and environmental costly production capacity, exceeding the target of 2014. In order to clean up the air, old cars and cars with yellow license plates, which indicate higher pollution, were disposed. The number of those cars disposed exceeded the annual target. The strategy of innovation driven development was adopted, efforts were made to streamline the process of commercializing the research findings, and the scope of the pilot Zhongguancun Science Park was expanded. Breakthroughs were made in major scientific projects such as supercomputing, lunar exploration and satellite application. The test flight for regional jets designed and manufactured by China was successful.

Agriculture as Foundation of Economy was Consolidated

Supportive policies for agriculture and farmers were stepped up in 2014 to consolidate the foundation of economy. Agricultural production has kept growing for 11 consecutive years. Farmers' income also has grown fast for 5 consecutive years. The annual grain output grew by 0.9%, or 5.16 million tons, to 607.1 million tons. Agricultural production capacity was enhanced steadily. Modern technology and machinery became more widely used. Major irrigation projects accelerated. Water efficient irrigation was provided to 2.23 million hectares of farmland. 230,000 kilometers of rural roads were built or renovated. A new round of returning farmland to forest and grassland was launched. Confirmation and certifying of land rights progressed smoothly. New types of agricultural operation entities grew fast.

Public Welfare Improving Continuously, Providing the Insurance Industry with Broader Room for Development

The Chinese government was dedicated to improving people's welfare in 2014, which expanded the room for development of the insurance industry.

Continuous Improvement of Living Standards

In 2014, urban and rural household income kept rising. The disposable income per capita grew by 8% in real terms. The urban citizens' disposable income per person amounted to RMB 28,844 Yuan, up by 6.8% in real terms. The rural population's disposable income per person was RMB 10,489 Yuan, which grew by 9.2% in real terms. Household consumption continued to grow. Total retail sales of consumer goods amounted to RMB 26 trillion Yuan, up by 10.9% in real terms, among which the retail sales in urban market grew 11.8% and that in rural market grew 12.9%. The sales volume of telecommunications equipment grew by 32.7%. Jewelry consumption was about the same with that of 2013. Furniture and cosmetics grew by more than 10%. Car sales went up by 7.7%. There were 83.07 million cars owned by civilians, 16.6% more YoY. Rural population in poverty decreased by 12.32 million. The government helped more than 66 million people in the rural areas to get hygiene water. Outbound tourists exceeded 100 million.

Strengthened Efforts in Protecting and Improving People's Livelihood

In 2014, China's employment continued to grow, with 13.22 million new jobs created in urban areas. As of the end of year, the registered unemployment rate in urban area was 4.09%. 7.4 million protection housing units commenced construction and 5.11 million units were completed. Education, science and technology, and culture undertakings continued to develop, with 621,000 graduate students and 7,214,000 college students enrolling at higher education institutions. The expenditure on research and development grew by 12.4% to RMB 1.3312 trillion Yuan. In the "people first" line of thinking, the government continued to increase the input in social welfare to provide basic protection to the people through different mechanisms. More than 70% of fiscal money was spent in areas concerning people's well-being.

Progress in the Construction of Social Security System

The social security level continued to increase. By the end of 2014, the number of urban employees covered by basic pension insurance and the number of urban and rural residents covered by basic pension insurance increased by 18.97 million and 3.57 million respectively. The number of people covered by basic medical insurance, unemployment insurance, work-related injury insurance and maternity insurance increased by 27.02 million, 6.26 million, 7.03 million and 6.43 million respectively. The "integration" of the new rural cooperative medical system and the urban resident basic medical system was launched. The basic pension benefit for enterprise retiree was 10% up. 13,109,000 urban residents received subsidy for medical insurance and 41,189,000 rural residents received subsidy for the new rural cooperative medical system. Temporary assistance system was built nationwide with the minimum standard raised by 9.97% and 14.1% for urban and rural residents respectively.

The Financial System Ran Steadily with Further Improved Capacities in Serving the Economy and Society

In 2014, China's financial markets continued healthy development, with policies on reform and development being steadily implemented. Financial markets played a bigger role in lowering funding cost and boosting real economy.

Prudent Monetary Policy and Comprehensive Deepening Reform and Opening up Financial Industry

In 2014, the People's Bank of China (PBC) continued to implement prudent monetary policy and expand its toolkit. It maintained an appropriate money supply and guided financial institutions to use its old funds and new funds more efficiently. Financial institutions were encouraged to support key sectors and important projects like agriculture, farmers and rural areas, small and microbusinesses, shanty towns renovation and railway construction by expanding their funding channels. M2 supply grew by 12.2% YoY. New RMB loans totaled RMB 9.78 trillionYuan, 890 billion higher than 2013. Social financing scale grew close to RMB 16.5 trillion Yuan. In terms of financial reform, key areas reform advanced to give the market a decisive role in resource allocation. Market-oriented reform of interest rate and exchange rate were further advanced. RMB was used more frequently in overseas transactions. Convertibility of capital account saw new progress. Substantial work has been done to establish deposit insurance.

The Banking Industry Ran Steadily

In 2014, operation and risk indicators of China's commercial banks improved, with steady growth of the balance sheet and overall stable capital adequate ratio. As of the end of 2014, the total asset of China's banking industry was RMB 172.3 trillion Yuan (+13.87% YoY). The commercial banks realized net profit of RMB 1.55 trillion Yuan (+9.65% YoY). The average rate of return on assets was 1.23%. The weighted average capital adequacy ratio of commercial banks was 13.18%, up by 0.99 percentage point compared with the beginning of 2014. The balance of non-performing loans increased by RMB 250.6 billion Yuan to RMB 842.6 billion Yuan. The non-performing loan ratio was 1.25%, up by 0.25 percentage point YoY.

Capital Market Developed Steadily and the Multi-layered Market System Made Groundbreaking Progress

China's capital market maintained the momentum of steady operation in 2014. Market-oriented reform of the infrastructure went deeper. M&A and delisting mechanisms were perfected. The pilot project to allow cross market stock investment by mainland and Hong Kong investors was officially launched. In 2014, the number of listed companies in the New Third Board exceeded 1500. A multi-layered capital market was taking shape. Listed companies raised RMB 839.7 billion Yuan from domestic markets, RMB 151.2 billion Yuan more than that of 2013. At the end of 2014, Shanghai Composite Index and Shenzhen Composite Index closed at 3,234 points and 1,415 points, up by 52.8% and 33.7% respectively. The index of growth enterprise market closed at 1,471 points with a rise of 12.8% YoY.

Insurance Market Realized Strong Growth with Further Improved Overall Capacity

In 2014, China's insurance industry grew fast, demonstrating vigor and vitality. The pricing reform went on smoothly, expecting universal insurance pricing reform and auto insurance pricing reform plans to come out very soon. Reform of market entry/exit mechanism deepened. Insurance asset allocation became more diversified. Progress has been made in the construction of catastrophe insurance system. China Risk Oriented Solvency System (C-ROSS) has taken shape. Protection of the interst of insurance cosumers gained new progress. The insurance industry's solvency surplus totaled RMB 720.7 billion Yuan. Only 1 insurer had inadequate solvency. Insurance premium income nationwide hit RMB 2 trillion Yuan (+17.5% YoY). Insurance total asset was more than RMB 10 trillion Yuan, 22.3% higher than the beginning of 2014.

Photos by staff of the insurance industry

Photos by staff of the insurance industry

03

Insurance Industry's Contribution to Economic and Social Development

- Enhancing Medical Insurance Protection for the Public
- Insurance Industry Supported the Multi-layered Old-age Security System
- Innovative Social Management
- Participation in Disaster Prevention and Assistance System
- Agriculture Insurance P ayed a Bigger Role
- The Insurance Industry Facilitating Economic Transformation
- An Industry with a Strong Sense of Social Responsibility

Enhancing Medical Insurance Protection for the Public

Major Illness Insurance for Urban and Rural Residents

2014 saw progress in major illness insurance for urban and rural residents as a part of the national medical insurance system. As of the end of 2014, major illness insurance was conducted in all provinces except Tibet. 16 insurers provide major illness insurance to 700 million people, or 70% of the population the product is designed to cover, in the 2,128 counties/districts of the 265 cities of 27 provinces. This includes the Xinjiang Production and Construction Corps. Premium income of major illness insurance yielded RMB 15.44 billion Yuan and 1.97 million claims were settled. The current biggest case is more than RMB 800,000 Yuan. The average payout per case was RMB 5,600 Yuan. The reimbursement proportion was about 70%, 10 to 15 percentage points higher than the basic medical insurance. The total payout of RMB 11.1 billion Yuan helped the sick so that they don't get into poverty because of medical bills.

Developing Commercial Health Insurance

Insurers can provide the public with better health risk protection through their commercial health insurance products to meet the needs that cannot be satisfied by basic medical insurance. More than 100 insurers conducted commercial health insurance in 2014, selling more than 2,300 products of illness insurance, medical expense insurance, long-term care insurance and disability income loss insurance. Commercial health insurance premium income totaled RMB 158.63 billion Yuan, up by 41.9% YoY. Claims payout was RMB 57.24 billion Yuan. Experiments were conducted to link health insurance with health management so as to expand insurance service from expense reimbursement and compensation to comprehensive health management for illness prevention, treatment and care. In this way, people's health was improved.

Managing Basic Medical Protection Plans

As an industry with a strong sense of social responsibility, the insurance industry accepted the entrustment of the government to participate in the management of basic medical insurance plans such as the new rural medical cooperative and basic medical insurance for urban and rural residents. By using its advantages in actuarial technology, professional service, and risk management, the insurance industry lowered the cost of such plans, controlled medical expenses, relieved the fiscal burden of the government, and improved the service quality and efficiency of basic medical insurance. As of the end of 2014, 320 million people received service from insurers in the basic medical insurance plans. The plans' funds entrusted with insurers increased by RMB 18.92 billion Yuan. 36.12 million cases amounting to RMB 13.52 billion Yuan were settled. Insurers also provided supplementary medical insurance for urban and rural residents, supplementary group medical insurance for businesses and organizations as well as medical assistance services, the premium income of which was RMB 14.53 billion Yuan and the reimbursement was RMB 14.45 billion Yuan.

> **Column 1   State Council Issued *Several Opinions on Accelerating the Development of Commercial Health Insurance***
>
> On Nov. 17, 2014, the State Council issued *Several Opinions on Accelerating the Development of Commercial Health Insurance,* a landmark document symbolizing a strategic, innovative, market-based and groundbreaking solution to the issue of public medical insurance protection in the "new normal".
>
> This document set out the guiding philosophy, goals and basic principles as well as supportive policies for the development of commercial health insurance for a long time to come. It required stronger leadership, better coordination among relevant ministries and departments and a supportive environment. It will have a far-reaching impact on the improvement of China's medical protection system, deepening of medical reform and the development of the health industry.

The Whole Guangdong Province Having Access to Major Illness Insurance

As of the end of 2014, major illness insurance was accessible in every place of Guangdong Province. Such insurance was organized and managed at municipal level to cover both urban residents and rural population. In 18 cities of Guangdong province, major illness insurance was underwritten by commercial insurers, covering more than 110 counties/ districts, protecting more than 60 million people. The effective link between the government and the market raised the reimbursement proportion by 14.3%. In this mechanism, people got more than half of their medical expenses covered.

Sunshine Insurance Got Approval for the First Insurer-invested Hospital

In May, 2014, Sunshine Insurance Group got approval to set up a hospital, which was the first joint-stock hospital in China invested by an insurer in cooperation with large state-owned hospitals and medical education institutions. The RMB 2.5 billion Yuan project covers 900,000 square meters. The 280,000 square meters of out-patient and in-patient buildings have been constructed. The hospital now has 2000 beds.

Insurance Industry Supported the Multi-layered Old-age Security System

In 2014, following the instructions of the State Council, CIRC achieved a lot in encouraging insurance industry to support the multi-layered old-age security system by making use of its expertise and management skills.

Pilot Projects to Participate in Basic Pension

Insurers were active participants in the management of basic pension. As of the end of 2014, insurers provided management services for the new rural medical cooperatives in Yixing of Jiangsu province; Jingyang District of Deyang, Sichuan province; Qujiang District of Quzhou, Zhejiang province; Chuzhou and Lianyungang of Jiangsu province, Shifang and Mianzhu of Sichuan province, covering about 1.32 million people.

The participation of insurers in the management of basic pension is a new way of operation that combines the leading role of the government and the operation role of the market to provide professional service to the public. It is an innovative and more efficient way of public service provision because the participation of insurers not only reduced the government's pressure of limited staff and administrative cost, but also introduced information-based management and professional risk control into the basic pension system.

2014 China Residents Retirement Preparedness Index released by Aegon-CNOOC and Qinghua University on June 25, 2014

Column 2   House for Pension Pilot Project Launched

In June, 2014, CIRC issued *Guidance on Pilot Projects of House for Pension*, deciding to launch the project in Beijing, Shanghai, Guangzhou and Wuhan as of July 1, 2014.

House for pension project is an innovative commercial pension product that combines mortgage with life annuity. The retirees with full ownership of their houses can mortgage their houses with insurers to get annuity till they pass away. During their retirement life, they maintain their rights to live in and use the houses, to receive earnings and to dispose the houses if the mortgagee agrees. When the retirees pass away, the insurers get the right to sell the house for the annuity payouts. By transferring homes into a source of pension, this product provides new opportunities for the insurance industry to play a role in old age security system.

New Risk Sharing Mechanism for Old Age Security in Suzhou

In 2014, explorations were carried out in Suzhou to establish a new risk sharing mechanism for old age security. The government there purchased nursing institution comprehensive liability insurance, home nurturing organization liability insurance and accident and injury insurance for the seniors, providing accident and injury protection amounting to RMB 10.6 billion Yuan to 625,000 seniors and risk protection totaling RMB 3.4 billion Yuan for 41,000 beds in 95 streets of Suzhou.

Management for Enterprise Annuities

Insurers were also trustees, account managers and investment managers for enterprise annuities, providing service throughout the establishment, operation and payout of these annuities by using their expertise in designing products and their experience with customers and prudent investment. As of the end of 2014, insurers were trustees of 43,000 businesses, covering 8.77 million people and assets amounting to RMB 317.42 billion Yuan. The percentage of enterprise annuity assets entrusted with insurers is 68.8% of all those assets entrusted with legal entities. Insurers managed 9,845 enterprise accounts and 2.52 million individual accounts. They also invested RMB 375.37 billion Yuan for the enterprise annuities, or about 50.7% of all those assets.

Commercial Annuity Promoted

Commercial insurance offers a variety of pension products and services and can be a very good supplement to social old age security. Currently, 69 insurers in China conduct commercial annuity business through a variety of products. Recently, annuity insurance has been growing fast with average annual growth rate of 16.9% between 2001 and 2014. In 2014, annuity insurance income registered RMB 282.2 billion Yuan (+77.2% YoY). There were 69.433 million in-force policies covering 100 million people, providing protection amounting to RMB 1.4 trillion Yuan.

Innovative Social Management

In 2014, liability insurance participated in innovative social management as an effective way to diversify social risks, mitigate conflicts, reduce government pressure and maintain social stability. For the whole year, liability insurance premium income was RMB 25.34 billion Yuan and the insured amount registered RMB 66.5 trillion Yuan.

Stepping up Medical Liability Insurance for Better Medical Dispute Settlement

Medical liability insurance is an important part of medical dispute prevention and settlement mechanism. It works together with dispute settlement channels to reduce conflict between the hospital and the patients' family over medical accidents so that the hospital can function normally. In 2014, CIRC, together with National Health and Family Planning Commission, Ministry of Finance and other 3 ministries issued *Opinions on Stepping up Medical Liability Insurance*. Together with National Health and Family Planning Commission, CIRC conducted a national inspection on the dispute settlement of hospitals.

Medical Liability Insurance Promoted in Tianjin

In 2014, CIRC Tianjin Bureau actively promoted the development of medical liability insurance as part of the national governance system and governance modernization efforts. *Regulation on Medical Dispute Settlement in Tianjin* was released, according to which, public hospitals above level II must purchase medical liability insurance. As of the end of 2014, the insurance industry provided to 81 hospitals with protection of RMB 590 million Yuan, settled 3,868 claims with payment of RMB 210 million Yuan. 87.5% of medical disputes were successfully settled.

Product Safety Liability Insurance Promoted for Safer Products

CIRC encouraged the development of product safety liability insurance as a part of market-oriented product safety accident assistance and accountability system. In 2014, CIRC in conjunction with National Administration of Quality Supervision, Inspection and Quarantine, issued *Notice on Conducting Product Safety Liability Insurance* to encourage the implementation of this insurance for special equipment and popular consumption goods. It protects the rights of the people, helps to maintain social harmony and safety as well as improves businesses' risk management.

Food Safety Liability Insurance Encouraged for Safer Foods and Drugs

In 2014, CIRC in conjunction with Food Safety Office of the State Council and China Food and Drug Administration issued *Guiding Opinions on Conducting Food Safety Liability Insurance,* taking the implementation of pilot project on this insurance into local governments'performance assessment system and including the participation of businesses into their credit record and rating system.

Hunan Province Carried out Food Safety Liability Insurance Pilot Project

In 2014, Hunan province promoted a pilot project of food safety liability insurance to manufacturers, canteens and catering businesses. 1,371 policies were issued, providing insurance amount of RMB 1.48 billion Yuan to 897 canteens, 417 manufacturers and 57 catering businesses.

Environmental Pollution Liability Insurance Boosted to Perfect Environmental Protection Mechanism

The year 2014 saw a big step forward for environmental pollution liability insurance as the newly revised *Environmental Protection Law* encourages businesses to buy this product. In conjunction with Ministry of Environmental Protection, CIRC issued *Guiding Opinions on Conducting Compulsory Environmental Pollution Liability Insurance Pilot Projects* in 2014 to launch pilot project of compulsory environment pollution liability insurance for high risk industries such as heavy metals and petrochemical industries. Risk assessment standards have been made for 6 industries such as chemical industry and metallurgy industry as part of the standard system for this insurance. Under the guidance of CIRC, the Insurance Association of China has issued example terms and clauses for this insurance.

Participation in Disaster Prevention and Assistance System

The Design of Catastrophe Mechanism has been Completed to Provide Legal Basis for Catastrophe Insurance

In 2014, CIRC, in conjunction with Ministry of Finance, drafted *Work Plan for the Establishment of Catastrophe Insurance to Better Use Insurance for Economic Compensation.* A taskforce was established to work on the design of catastrophe insurance. The taskforce completed *Research Report on the Establishment of Catastrophe Insurance* and *Operation Plan for China's Earthquake Catastrophe Insurance,* which means the top level design of catastrophe insurance in China has been completed.

Based on China's realities and the needs for catastrophe insurance, CIRC picked earthquake insurance to break the ground. It drafted *Earthquake Catastrophe Insurance Rules,* which state clearly that catastrophe insurance will be operated through cooperation between the government and the market. The *Rules* also define the rights and obligations of all parties involved, how catastrophe insurance will be organized, how the key institution will be established and the operation rules and risk control requirements. The *Rules* provide a legal basis for catastrophe insurance in China.

Pilot Project Carried out for Implementation of Earthquake Insurance

In 2014, CIRC actively advanced earthquake insurance by developing example product, providing necessary infrastructure and improving risk diversification mechanism. A national household earthquake insurance example product was developed, which covers as many urban and rural houses as possible. The protection it provides is basic and insurance amount is different for urban and rural houses. An insurance pool was organized with a work plan and charter in place. Research in the viability of establishing an earthquake catastrophe insurance fund has been carried out. The idea is to collect a certain percentage of earthquake insurance premium or underwriting profit surplus and put that into the fund. The fund will be put under custody before a special management entity is established. The fund will be managed separately to accumulate interest and will be used centrally across the country.

Pilot Projects Carried Out as a Way of Accumulating Experience for Full Implementation of Catastrophe Insurance

Pilot projects were expanded from Shenzhen to Ningbo. The catastrophe insurance system in Ningbo is composed of three parts, namely, public catastrophe insurance, catastrophe fund and commercial catastrophe insurance, among which public catastrophe insurance covers home damage for the first time. Besides Ningbo, other places such as Yunnan, Shanghai and Guangdong also worked on pilot project plans reflecting local features.

China Insurance's Rural Home Pilot Project

In 2014, China Insurance implemented a pilot rural home insurance project in 11 districts/counties of Chengdu, the capital of Sichuan province. This project covered 15 risks including earthquake, storm, flood, fire and others. The participation ratio was close to 30% at the end of 2014, providing RMB 27.2 billion Yuan's insurance protection to 450,000 rural households.

> **Champion P&C Insurance Establishing Catastrophe Risk Management Research Center with Yunnan University of Finance and Economics**
>
> December of 2014 saw the opening of Catastrophe Risk Management Research Center founded by Champion P&C Insurance and Yunnan University of Finance and Economics. This center is an open research and development platform, a think tank, an innovation incubator to support the business development and talent training for catastrophe insurance.

Agriculture Insurance Played a Bigger Role

In 2014, agriculture insurance, benefiting from policies supporting agriculture and farmers, kept the momentum of steady and fast development, playing a positive role in ensuring stable agricultural production, enhancing the resilience of farmers against disasters, stabilizing farmers' income and safeguarding national food security.

Constantly Expanding Coverage

Premium income for agricultural insurance was RMB 32.58 billion Yuan, up by 6.3% YoY. The number of rural households insured totaled 250 million, up by 15.7% YoY. The amount insured exceeded RMB 1.6 trillion Yuan, up by 17.7% YoY. The claims payment totaled RMB 21.46 billion Yuan, up by 2.9% YoY. 32.45 million farmers were benefited from agriculture insurance, up by 2.1% YoY. 47.7% of staple crops area, or 78 million hectares were insured. The participation ratios of the three major grain crops, i.e. corn, rice and wheat, were 68.7%, 69.5% and 49.3% respectively. 144.67 million hectares of forests, or 67.2% of forests in China were insured. 130 million hogs and 3.981 million cows were insured, up by 54.3% and 21.2% respectively.

Better Compliance

In 2014, CIRC together with Ministry of Finance conducted a comprehensive inspection on agricultural insurance. 11 P&C legal entities were inspected. Through the inspection, fake agricultural underwriting and claims settlement were prevented to make sure that fiscal subsidies were properly used to really benefit the farmers.

Better Infrastructure

In 2014, CIRC stepped up infrastructure construction for agricultural insurance. It cancelled licensing requirements for agricultural insurance business to increase competition. It issued *Notice on Improving Clauses of Agriculture Insurance Fiscally Subsidized by Central Government* with Ministry of Finance and Ministry of Agriculture to strengthen regulation on clauses and pricing, making premium rates and insurance amount more flexible. National Agriculture Insurance Information Platform was initiated to facilitate China Reinsurance Pool for Agriculture Insurance.

> **Column 3   China Reinsurance Pool for Agriculture Insurance**
>
> On November 21, 2014, China Reinsurance Pool for Agriculture Insurance was founded. It was initiated by 23 insurers with agriculture insurance license and China Re. The pool covers all of the agriculture insurance products. Its establishment improved the risk transfer mechanism for agricultural catastrophes by providing a stable channel for risk transfer.

Better Policy Environment

In 2014, the central government increased fiscal subsidies for agriculture insurance by 20%. CIRC, Ministry of Finance and State Administration of Taxation agreed to extend income tax incentives for agriculture insurance to the end of 2016. The subsidization percentage of hog insurance was raised from 10% to 50%. Cow insurance subsidization was expanded to 4 more provinces. Hog insurance subsidization was expanded to 2 more provinces. Forest insurance subsidization was expanded to another 2 provinces. Target price insurance was carried out on a trial basis in 20 provinces and cities.

First *Report on Survey of Agriculture Insurance Needs*

On September 10, 2014, the Insurance Society of China released *Report on Survey of Agriculture Insurance Needs*. Based on more than 10,000 samples, the report analyzed the risk profiles of farmers, agricultural economy organizations and local governments in China. It gave advice concerning how to further improve supportive policies for agriculture insurance, how to increase participation and coverage of agriculture insurance and how to optimize relevant service system and provide higher-quality services.

Vegetable Weather Index Insurance Launched by Anxin

In 2014, Anxin Agricultural Insurance launched vegetable weather index insurance in its explorations of applying weather index in their products. This new product is based on the index of damages caused by different weather conditions and compensates the insured when triggered. Needing no sophisticated technologies in claims settlement and having simple procedures, this product has low cost of management. The insured know that they are going to get the compensation when they read the weather index released. In this way, there is no more information asymmetry, adverse selection or moral hazard. This product has provided insurance amount of RMB 6.55 billion Yuan to 32 agricultural cooperatives. By compensating farmers for their loss through a timely manner, the farmers' motivation to grow vegetables was protected.

The Insurance Industry Facilitating Economic Transformation

Under the "new normal", better quality and higher efficiency are the keys to economic development. In 2014, the insurance industry stepped up its efforts to facilitate real economy development and economic transformation and upgrading, implementing the instructions of CPC Central Committee and State Council.

Insurance Assets Supporting Economic Construction

As of the end of 2014, the insurance industry provided more than RMB 1 trillion Yuan in financing for infrastructure projects such as transportation, energy, railway and irrigation and public welfare projects such as shanty town renovation, protection housing and nursing communities. The insurance industry initiated 378 debt plans, equity plans and asset-backed plans with registered amount totaling RMB 1.06444 trillion Yuan.

The insurance industry expanded its investment from infrastructure debt plans to stock ownership plans, asset-backed plans and equity investment funds. Investment portfolio also expanded from single asset class such as debt or equity to more flexible portfolios such as debt and equity mixed or preferred stock to better meet the diversified needs of financing.

Column 4 *Guiding Opinions on Insurance Industry Serving New Urbanization*

In March 2014, to implement the spirit of the CPC Central Committee's Working Meeting on Urbanization and the *New Urbanization Plan (2014–2020)* issued by the State Council, CIRC issued *Guiding Opinions on Insurance Industry Serving New Urbanization*. The *Opinions* asks the industry players to develop commercial pension and health insurance, to carry out explorations in asset management, to protect the sustainable development of urban economy, to strengthen risk management for safer cities, to provide better agriculture insurance products and better services so as to support new urbanization.

PICC Founded the First Government-Financial SOE Equity Fund

An RMB 12.1 billion Yuan equity fund to develop east, west and north Guangdong was founded by PICC. It is the first cooperation fund between provincial government and financial SOE. The focus of this fund is to finance urbanization projects in Guangdong.

Credit Guarantee Insurance Encouraged to Support Micro Financing

Working together with Ministry of Industry and Information Technology, Ministry of Commerce, People's Bank of China and CBRC, CIRC drafted guidance on developing credit guarantee insurance to support micro businesses. Credit guarantee insurance can enhance credit rating and increase loans for micro businesses to relieve their financing difficulties. The guidance encourages banks to give favorable loans to micro businesses that have credit insurance and loan guarantee insurance. Insurance companies with a certain size of business in this area can be linked to PBC's credit reporting system for information sharing.

In 2014, based on the experience of a pilot project in Ningbo, more micro loans guarantee insurance projects were promoted nationwide. The government, the banks and the insurers all had their own roles to play in this insurance mechanism. The government provided guidance, the insurers operated the business and the risks were shared. From 2009 to the end of 2014, 48 cities/districts of 21 provinces (including autonomous regions and municipalities directly under the central government) carried out this type of pilot projects. 9 provinces/autonomous regions such as Zhejiang, Guangxi and Yunnan issued relevant guidance. These projects helped 84,000 micro businesses to get loans amounting to RMB 22.9 billion Yuan in 2014.

On Sep. 18, 2014, CIRC and Ningbo Municipal Government co-organized a meeting to disseminate Ningbo's experience of insurance supporting SMEs. Chairman Xiang Junbo, Vice Chairman Chen Wenhui and the government leaders of Ningbo attended the meeting. 4 ministries/departments/commissions including Ministry of Industry and Information Technology and CBRC as well as 12 provincial offices of financial affairs took part in it.

Short-term Export Credit Insurance Promoted to Help Domestic Businesses to "Go Global"

Short-term export credit insurance can protect export enterprises from default risks and enhance their international competitiveness. In 2013, based on experiences of other countries, CIRC together with Ministry of Finance and Ministry of Commerce started to introduce 4 insurers to conduct short-term export credit insurance on a trial basis. In 2014, the short-term export credit insurance realized a premium income of USD 1.18 billion, offered USD 360.2 billion of amount insured and supported over 53,000 export enterprises to get RMB 212.58 billion Yuan in financing, including 37,000 micro export enterprises to get RMB 25.23 billion Yuan in financing.

An Industry with a Strong Sense of Social Responsibility

In 2014, in the spirit of "one for all, all for one", the insurance industry proactively fulfilled its social responsibilities through engagement in social charity and public undertakings such as education, environmental protection and disaster assistance.

Column 5   First *Chinese Insurance Industry Social Responsibilities Whitepaper* Released

July 8, 2014, witnessed the first *Chinese Insurance Industry Social Responsibilities Whitepaper* released by CIRC. It takes stock of the functions and roles the insurance industry has played in economic transformation, social security, disaster assistance and social management innovation. It also displays the development and achievement in agriculture insurance, catastrophe insurance, liability insurance and major illness insurance in recent years, and fully shows what the insurance industry has contributed to the society.

China Life Actively Engaged in Charity Activities

In 2014, China Life Charity Fund donated RMB 36 million Yuan. The money was used to help orphans of Wenchuan earthquake, Yushu earthquake and Quzhou mudslide, to sponsor poverty alleviation projects in Yunxi County of Hubei province, Tiandeng County and Longzhou County of Guangxi province. It was also used to help families that had lost their only child, establish kidney dialysis facilities for local clinics in rural areas of Liaoning province, buy ambulances and type-B color ultrasonic equipment for township hospitals in the mountains of Southern Ningxia Autonomous Region as well as fund cancer censure and buy critical disease insurance for women in poor regions.

Taikang Pension and Guahao.com Launched an Insurance Plan for Doctors

On October 18, 2014, in cooperation with Guahao.com, Taikang Pension launched an insurance plan for doctors called "No More Worries". It provided doctors with accident injury insurance with insured amount of RMB 50,000 Yuan and accident medical insurance with insured amount of RMB 5,000 Yuan. It attracted more than 10,000 doctors. Doctors who registered at Guahao.com can apply for this plan on Guahao.com website or through mobile phone apps.

Huaxia Insurance Supported Anti-Japanese War Veterans

Huaxia Insurance cofounded Huaxia Charity with China Youth Development Foundation and China Ageing Development Foundation. Huaxia Charity donated more than RMB 2.6 million Yuan to a charity project that supported Anti-Japanese War veterans. Charity workers looked for the veterans, gave them allowances, honorary certificates and medals. They also interviewed and videotaped the veterans giving oral accounts of history.

Anbang Pension Visited Nursing Homes in Double Ninth Festival

During the Double Ninth Festival, a festival for seniors, Anbang Pension employees worked as volunteers in 10 nursing homes in Beijing and Tianjin. These volunteers brought laptops, blood pressure meters, blood glucose meters and cooking oil for nearly 1,000 seniors in the nursing homes.

Liberty Mutual's Traffic Safety Project for Children

In 2014, Liberty Mutual sponsored traffic safety education activities for Children in Jinhua, Beijing, Jinan and Guangzhou. This project, since 2012, has organized activities in many cities.

Photos by staff of the insurance industry

Photos by staff of the insurance industry

04

Insurance Regulation

General Information

Main Responsibilities

1. Formulating policies, strategies and plans regarding the development of the insurance industry, drafting relevant laws and regulations regarding insurance supervision and regulation, and making relevant rules for the insurance industry.

2. Examining and approving the establishment of insurance companies and their branches, insurance groups and insurance holding companies; approving the establishment of insurance asset management companies in conjunction with relevant authorities; examining and approving the establishment of representative offices by overseas insurance institutions within the territory of China; examining and approving the establishment of insurance intermediaries, such as agencies, brokerages, loss-adjusting companies and their branches; examining and approving the establishment of overseas insurance institutions by domestic insurance and non-insurance institutions; examining and approving the merger, split, alteration and dissolution of insurance institutions; deciding whether or not to take over an insurance company or designating an organization to take it over; organizing or participating in the bankruptcy and liquidation process of insurance companies.

3. Examining and confirming the qualifications of senior managerial personnel in all insurance-related institutions; establishing the basic qualification standards for insurance practitioners.

4. Examining and approving the clauses and premium rates of insurance types related to public interests, statutory insurance types and newly developed life insurance types; filing the insurance clauses and premium rates of other insurance types.

5. Supervising the solvency and market conduct of insurance companies in accordance with the law; managing the insurance security fund and monitoring the insurance guarantee deposits; formulating rules and regulations on insurance fund management on the basis of laws and relevant policies of the State, and supervising insurance fund management in accordance with the law.

6. Supervising business operation of policy-oriented insurance and statutory insurance; supervising organizational forms and operations, such as captive insurance and mutual insurance; conducting administration of associations and institutions of the insurance industry, such as the Insurance Association of China and the Insurance Institute of China.

7. Conducting investigations into the following irregularities and imposing penalties according to law: unfair competition and other irregularities by insurance institutions and practitioners, direct engagement or disguised engagement in the insurance business by non-insurance institutions.

8. Supervising overseas insurance institutions established by domestic insurance and non-insurance institutions in accordance with the law.

9. Laying down standards for the information system of the insurance industry; establishing insurance risk assessment, risk warning and risk monitoring systems; following, analyzing, monitoring and predicting the operation of the insurance market; compiling the statistics and report forms of the insurance industry and disclosing them in accordance with relevant regulations of the State.

10. Taking on other duties commissioned by the State Council.

Organizational Structure of CIRC

General Office

Development and Reform Department

Policy Research Department

Finance and Accounting Department

Vice Chairman

Insurance Consumer Interests Protection Bureau

Secretary of Discipline

Property Insurance Regulatory Department

Life Insurance Regulatory Department

Vice Chairman

Insurance Intermediary Regulatory Department

Chairman

Insurance Fund Management Regulatory Department

Vice Chairman

International Departmant

Legal Affairs Department

Vice Chairman

Statistics and IT Department

Inspection Bureau

Assistant Chairman

Human Resources Department

Disciplinary Inspection Department

Party Committee of CIRC Head Office

Based on the authorized administrative functions, the 36 branches directly affiliated to CIRC, as well as insurance regulatory sub-branches in Tangshan of Hebei Province, Suzhou of Jiangsu Province, Wenzhou of Zhejiang Province, Yantai of Shandong Province and Shantou of Guangdong Province, regulate the insurance markets within their respective jurisdictions, maintain the steady operation of local insurance markets and promote the sustainable and healthy development of the insurance industry in line with laws, regulations, guidelines and policies.

Regulation Objectives

- Protect consumer rights and interests
- Prevent and mitigate market risks
- Promote the sustainable and healthy development of the insurance industry

Regulation on Corporate Governance

In 2014, CIRC continued to push forward the reform of corporate governance, constantly strengthened and improved relevant regulation, and achieved positive results in mechanism construction, regulatory measures upgrade and group company supervision.

Constantly Improving Corporate Governance

CIRC promulgated *Measures on Evaluation of Insurance Company Corporate Governance,* to rate insurers according to their corporate governance, link the rating result to the remuneration supervision, branch application and business inspection of the company to make the evaluation more binding, and give a yellow/red card to those with poor corporate governance and no effective improvement. CIRC promulgated *Notice on Further Regulating Affiliated Transaction of Insurance Companies,* to further prevent the actual controller of an insurance company from embezzling the interest of medium and small shareholders and the policy holders through affiliated party transactions by strengthening proportion regulation, internal review and information disclosure. A database of insurance company corporate governance problems was set up as an important reference for corporate governance evaluation and on-site inspection.

Constantly Improving On-site and Off-site Supervision of Corporate Governance

CIRC continued to carry out corporate regulation inspection and further expanded the scale of inspection target, scope and frequency. According to the inspection result, regulation letters were sent to relevant companies to urge them to make changes. In terms of off-site supervision, CIRC continued to analyze the insurers' annual reports of corporate governance and sent risk warning letters to urge faulty companies to make changes. CIRC also conducted a theme inspection on the articles of incorporation of 88 insurers, and urged rectification within a time limit.

Comprehensively Monitoring and Preventing Group Operation Risks

CIRC released *Interim Measures on Regulation of Non-insurance Subsidiaries of Insurance Companies,* to implement overall risk monitoring on the non-insurance subsidiaries of insurance companies to prevent cross-company and cross-sector risk transfer. CIRC promoted the regulation of Domestic Systemically Important Insurers (D-SII), to gradually establish a D-SII supervision system that was internationally comparable and reflecting Chinese features. CIRC also released *Guidance on Consolidated Supervision of Insurance Groups* to clarify the responsibility of consolidated supervision. The infrastructure of group supervision was strengthened with improved reporting mechanism and sound filing management to consolidate the foundation of off-site group supervision.

Column 6   CIRC Released *Interim Measures on Regulation of Non-insurance Subsidiaries of Insurance Companies*

In September 2014, CIRC released *Interim Measures on Regulation of Non-insurance Subsidiaries of Insurance Companies,* to enhance regulation on and improve risk monitor mechanism of non-insurance subsidiaries of insurance companies. The *Measures* mainly regulate five actions that insurance companies make in investing in and managing their non-insurance subsidiaries: the first action is investing in and setting the non-insurance subsidiaries; the second is management of the non-insurance subsidiary; the third is internal transaction with the non-insurance subsidiary; the forth is the outsourcing to the non-insurance subsidiary; the fifth is the risk firewall between the insurance company and the non-insurance subsidiary. The *Measures* set specific rules on the criteria of insurance companies entering non-insurance business, the exit of insurance companies from non-insurance business, and the reporting mechanism.

Column 7   The Release of *Guidance on Consolidated Supervision of Insurance Groups*

In December 2014, CIRC released *Guidance on Consolidated Supervision of Insurance Groups,* to further enhance insurance group supervision, improve the consolidated supervision of insurance groups, and effectively prevent operational risks of insurance groups. Based on the objective of effective prevention of insurance group risks, while supporting the group operation, group synergy and scale effect, the *Guidance* implemented overall risk monitoring over the insurance group through clarifying group structure, monitoring internal transaction, improving the overall risk management system and risk firewall mechanism, and improving corporate governance and information disclosure mechanism.

Column 8   Supervision of Global Systemically Important Insurers

In 2014, Ping An was re-selected as one of the global systemically important insurers (G-SII). CIRC established a crisis management team to guide Ping An in working out its risk resolution plans and systemic risk management plans. At the same time, supervision of D-SII also advanced with the supervisory framework and documents being drafted. The goal was to establish an internationally consistent and recognized system that can reflect the features of the Chinese market.

Solvency Regulation

Sufficient Solvency as a Whole

By the end of 2014, the overall solvency status of the insurance industry was sufficient, with only one insurance company below the solvency standard, and the other companies above 150%, which laid a solid foundation for the transition period of C-ROSS. The median of the solvency ratio of non-life insurance companies is 360%, up by 7 percentage points YoY; the median of life insurance companies is 285%, up by 21 percentage points YoY.

Solvency Surplus Increased Significantly

By the end of 2014, the solvency surplus of insurance industry was RMB 720.7 billion Yuan, RMB 165.6 billion Yuan or 30% higher than the beginning of the year. The increase of the solvency surplus was mainly due to the good performance of investment. In 2014, the return of insurance fund investment was RMB 535.88 billion Yuan, up by 46.5% YoY, a record high in the last five years. At the same time, in the fourth quarter of 2014, 17 companies increased their capital by RMB 30.45 billion Yuan.

Daily On-going Solvency Supervision Stepped Up

In 2014, CIRC further strengthened daily on-going solvency supervision, formulated solvency reporting rules concerning minimum capital of high cash-value products, blue chip stock investment, mutual fund investment and wealth management product investment of the old high-interest policies, in order to control the risks of high cash-value products, the negative spread risks of the high interest policies and insurance fund investment risks. CIRC suspended property investment value reassessment and carried out a review of the investment properties to prevent relevant risks. Efforts were made to improve quarterly solvency analysis and monitoring, and to upgrade the procedure of CIRC solvency regulatory committee to increase efficiency.

The Capital Increase Mechanism of Insurance Industry was Further Improved

In 2014, CIRC drafted *Administrative Measures on Capital Increase of Insurance Companies (for Consultation)* to set up a well-supervised multi-layered capital increase mechanism that uses different instruments. Eight major capital increase channels including common stock, preferred stock, capital reserves, etc. were allowed. The capital of an insurance company were divided into four categories, i.e. tier I capital, tier II capital, supplement I capital and supplement II capital, each with its own characteristics, criteria and required amount. CIRC supported the innovation in capital increase, reached out to relevant government department to discuss the feasibility of and ways to broaden financing channel for insurance companies. *Notice of CIRC on Insurance Companies Issuing Preferred Stocks* and *Announcement of PBOC and CIRC on Insurance Companies Issuing Capital Supplement Bond* were drafted.

Market Conduct Supervision

In face of the extremely complex internal and external situation in 2014, CIRC insisted on strict risk prevention, strengthened market conduct supervision, carried out new on-site inspection methods, straightened up the market, and achieved the goal of preventing regional and systemic risks.

Overall Reinforcement of On-site Inspection

In 2014, CIRC sent 2,586 teams to inspect 2,739 insurance institutions and intermediaries. According to the inspection results, 455 institutions and intermediaries and 529 persons received administrative sanctions, including disqualification of 24 persons, revoking the license of 13 institutions, forbidding the new business of 11 institutions. Besides, 776 insurance institutions and 350 persons were talked to by the regulators, received a notice of criticism or a letter from the regulator.

Special Inspection in Three Major Areas

First, an inspection on agriculture insurance was jointly conducted by CIRC and Ministry of Finance, covering 166 branches/subsidiaries of 11 non-life insurance companies. This inspection was mainly focused on irregularities such as false underwriting and false claims that infringed the interests of the state and the farmers. Second, nationwide inspection on the compliance of major illness insurance was carried out. With 3 parent-company inspection teams and 30 province-level teams, adopting large scale geographical cross examination for the first time, focusing on 121 major illness insurance programs, this inspection reviewed the operation of major illness insurance since the launching of this pilot project to make sure that this policy actually benefited the people. Third, overall inspection of insurance intermediary market, covering 135 insurance companies, 1,745 province branches, 2,530 full-time insurance intermediaries and 617 part-time insurance intermediaries was carried out. These unprecedented large scale theme inspections established the authority of CIRC and contained irregularities.

> **CIRC Shanxi Bureau Strengthened Inspection in County-level Market**
>
> CIRC Shanxi Bureau conducted well-focused quarterly inspections in county-level market, covering all 119 counties in Shanxi Province. Through the inspection, Shanxi Bureau was able to fully understand the situation in the county-level market. Seeing that agriculture insurance and major illness insurance were in great need, the Bureau encouraged expansion of the supply of these two products.

On-going Supervision to Mitigate Case Risks

In 2014, CIRC took strong measures to mitigate major case risks. Efforts were made to spot illegal behaviors before they got worse. 65 life insurance companies were investigated for fund misuse. Through information sharing of typical cases and exchange of experience, the regulators were able to better resolve similar cases. During the investigations, 17 persons were detained so that they cannot transfer money or escape to other countries. After the investigations, punishments were given to warn others. Under the guidance of CIRC, the market players have held 403 persons in 151 cases accountable. This increased the senior management's sense of responsibility and awareness of risk prevention. Over 30 major cases were investigated and based on the problems found in those cases, 10 insurance companies were asked to fix the loopholes in their company management procedure.

Steady Progress of "Anti-fraud, Anti-money Laundering and Anti-illegal Fund Raising" Campaign

"Anning Action" jointly carried out by CIRC and the police department in Zhejiang Province, Fujian Province, Ningbo City and Xiamen City, provided 5,599 clues of insurance fraud to the police and assisted the police to detect 184 fraud crimes with amount of near RMB 19 million Yuan and 29 criminal groups. The third Cross-Strait Anti Insurance Fraud Seminar was held in Xi'an with the theme of "Anti Insurance Fraud in Big Data Age", in which experience in anti insurance fraud with big data technology was shared. The MOU between CIRC, Office of the Commissioner of Insurance of Hong Kong and Monetary Authority of Macao on anti-fraud was signed in Macao. The anti-money laundering mechanism of insurance industry took shape, and special inspections were carried out on four insurance institutions. *Guidance for Insurance Institutes on Risk Assessment and Client Rating of Money Laundering and Terrorist Financing* was released to guide insurance institutions to rate their clients by money laundering risks. CIRC organized the insurance industry to conduct examination on illegal fund raising activities, launched "Anti-illegal Fund Raising Awareness Month", sent out 1.45 million pamphlets and reached out to over 10 million people.

Insurance Legal System Construction

In 2014, CIRC continued to reinforce and improve the legal system. The four-layered insurance legal system with the *Insurance Law,* insurance administrative rules, regulations, and guidance has taken shape, providing a solid foundation for the sustainable, healthy and fast growth of the insurance industry.

Completing the Implementation Assessment of *Insurance Law* to Promote the Revision of *Insurance Law*

In June 2014, CIRC completed the assessment on the implementation of *Insurance Law* and set the principle and priority of revision. In July 2014, CIRC launched the revision of *Insurance Law*. The revised draft was released for consultation in the insurance industry and among some academic experts at the end of 2014, for further research and improvement.

Revising Rules, Regulations and Measures

In 2014, CIRC revised and released

◆ *Administrative Rules on the Qualification of Director, Supervisor and Senior Managerial Personnel of Insurance Companies*

◆ *Measures for Administrative Approval of CIRC*

◆ *Interim Measures on Insurance Fund Management* and

◆ *Administrative Measures on Insurance Company Equity Shares*

Strengthening the Management of Regulatory Documents

In the first half of 2014, CIRC reviewed all the regulatory documents in force. Based on the principle of "unification, market-orientation, and efficiency", CIRC pushed forward the promulgation, revision and annulment of regulatory documents for a more up-to-date and organized regulatory document system.

International Cooperation and Communication

In 2014, CIRC continued to strengthen its cooperation with international organizations including the International Association of Insurance Supervisors (IAIS), the International Organization of Pension Supervisors (IOPS), the Asian Development Bank (ADB) and the Access to Insurance Initiative (A2ii), proactively participated in Asian Forum of Insurance Regulators(AFIR) and was elected as Forum Chairman, expanded bilateral exchanges with major countries (regions), and explored cooperation on themes such as cross-border supervision, pension, health insurance, solvency and investment regulation. CIRC has established and improved insurance regulatory cooperation mechanism with the United States, the European Union, Canada, United Kingdom, France, Australia, Thailand, Isle of Man, etc. CIRC also continued to cooperate with Hong Kong, Macao and Chinese Taipei on financial services. CIRC has widely participated in international insurance standard setting, exchange activities and construction of regional cooperation platform. Based on the situation of insurance industry development and opening up, CIRC participated in a number of multilateral negotiation mechanisms in coordination with national overall foreign strategy. These mechanisms promoted information sharing and exchange among regulators, and prevented cross-border risk transfer. The international cooperation and communication played a positive role in promoting China's insurance regulation, expanding its international influence, and maintaining the sustainable and healthy development of the Chinese insurance industry.

Human Resources and Information System

Human Resources

As of the end of 2014, CIRC had 2,835 employees, including 383 at head office, 2,452 at local branches. Among them, 1,717 were male and 1,118 were female, accounting for 61% and 39% respectively; 99% of the employees hold Bachelor degrees or above; 2,547 employees were under the age of 45, accounting for 90%.

In 2014, CIRC intensified its effort in training. The *2014-2018 Plan on Training of Insurance Regulators* was promulgated, three sessions of training programs for directors general were held to learn and implement the important remarks of Party Secretary General Xi Jinping.

Information System Upgrade

Improvement and Innovation

In 2014, CIRC reorganized the Information Work Committee, set up its working procedure, and pushed forward information upgrade. The standardization of insurance industry was further promoted with the revision of ten standards such as the *Standard of Insurance E-Commerce Platform* and the *Insurance Terminology.* Remote inspection was conducted to ten insurance companies for the first time, providing the basis for establishment of off-site risk regulation and assessment IT system.

Progress in Regulatory Information System

In 2014, CIRC strengthened the development and upgrade of regulatory information system by setting up 6 IT systems including human resources evaluation system and intermediary market review system, upgrading 4 systems including electronic file transfer system. Based on the framework of "two cities and three centers", CIRC completed the planning and construction of data backup center in Nanjing, conducted a feasibility research of constructing same-city main data center, and made solid progress in the construction of "two cities and three centers" modern insurance information framework.

Photos by staff of the insurance industry

Photos by staff of the insurance industry

05

Market Performance

- Non-life Insurance Market
- Life Insurance Market
- Insurance Intermediaries Market
- Insurance Fund Investment
- Professional Reinsurance Market
- Opening up of the Chinese Insurance Market

In 2014, China's insurance industry achieved premium income of RMB 2.02 trillion Yuan (+17.5% YoY). The insurance penetration and density were 3.18% and RMB 1,479.3 Yuan respectively. Insurance companies paid out RMB 719.44 billion Yuan (+15.9% YoY). The total assets of insurance companies amounted to RMB 10.2 trillion Yuan, a 22.3% increase from the start of the year.

Non-life Insurance Market

Stable Growth of Premium Income

In 2014, non-life insurance companies achieved premium income of RMB 754.61 billion Yuan, up by 16.4% YoY while down by 0.8 percentage point from 2013. Premium income of auto insurance reached RMB 551.59 billion Yuan, up by 16.8% YoY, while premium income of non-auto insurance reached RMB 203.02 billion Yuan, up by 15.3% YoY.

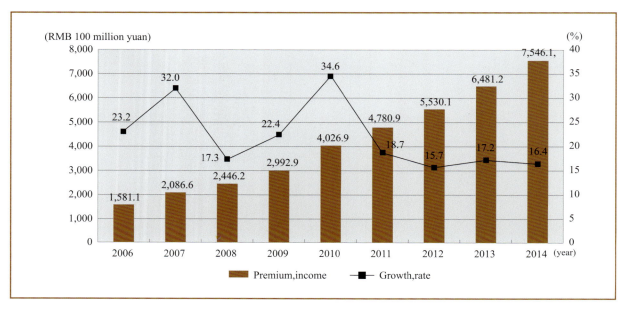

Chart 1   Premium Income and Growth Rate of Non-life Insurance Companies during 2006-2014

The top 5 contributors of 2014 non-life premium income were auto insurance (RMB 551.59 billion Yuan), commercial property insurance (RMB 38.74 billion Yuan), agricultural insurance (RMB 32.58 billion Yuan), liability insurance (RMB 25.34 billion Yuan) and credit insurance (RMB 20.07 billion Yuan), which altogether accounted for 88.6% of the market total.

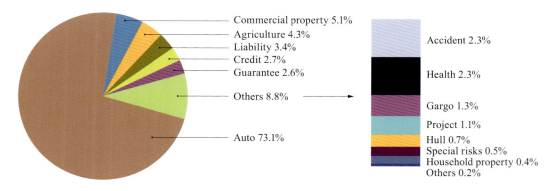

Chart 2   Portfolio of Non-life Insurance Business in 2014

Most of the non-life insurance lines maintained stable growth, including auto (+16.8% YoY), liability (+16.9% YoY), credit (+29.3% YoY), guarantee (+66.1% YoY), accident (+14.1% YoY) and health (+44.5% YoY).

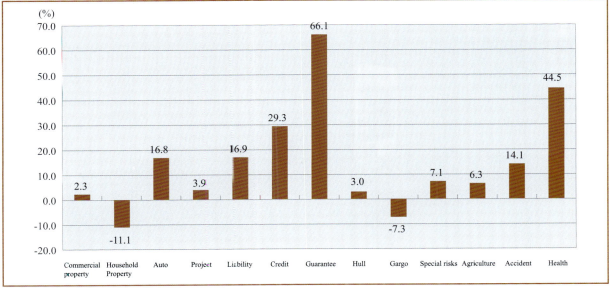

Chart 3 Premium Growth of Major Lines of Non-life Insurance in 2014

Industry Capacity Reinforced Significantly

In 2014, total assets of non-life insurance companies amounted to RMB 1.4 trillion Yuan, up by 26.9% YoY, and 10.5 percentage points higher than the growth rate of premium income. The net assets amounted to RMB 384.06 billion Yuan, up by 52.9% YoY, 36.5 percentage points higher than that of premium income.

Market Concentration Increased

As of the end of 2014, there were 67 non-life insurance companies in the market, among which 45 were domestic companies and 22 were foreign invested companies. The market share of the top 5 companies accounted for 74.7% (by premium income), up by 0.4 percentage point from a year earlier.

Table 1 Top 10 Non-life Insurance Companies by Premium Income in 2014

Rank	Name	Capital Structure	Premium Income(RMB billion Yuan)	Market Share (%)
1	PICC Property and Casualty Company Limited	Domestic	252.42	33.4
2	Ping An Property and Casualty Insurance of China, Ltd.	Domestic	142.86	18.9
3	China Pacific Property Insurance Co., Ltd.	Domestic	92.84	12.3
4	China Life Property and Casualty Insurance Company Limited	Domestic	40.40	5.4
5	China United Property Insurance Company Limited	Domestic	34.87	4.6
6	China Continent Property & Casualty Insurance Company Ltd.	Domestic	22.36	3.0
7	Sunshine Property and Casualty Insurance Co., Ltd.	Domestic	21.17	2.8
8	China Export & Credit Insurance Corporation	Domestic	18.12	2.4
9	Taiping General Insurance Co., Ltd.	Domestic	13.27	1.8
10	Tian An Insurance Co., Ltd.	Domestic	11.15	1.5
	Total		649.46	86.1

Underwriting Profit Back to Growth

In 2014, non-life insurance companies achieved underwriting profits of RMB 4.26 billion Yuan, up by 93.5% YoY. Auto insurance had underwriting loss of RMB 1.19 billion Yuan, 2.07 billion Yuan less compared with 2013. The whole industry achieved net profit of RMB 52.05 billion Yuan, up by 94% from a year earlier which benefited from the significant increase of investment return.

Risks Kept Under Control

At the end of 2014, the solvency and core capital ratio of all non-life insurance companies were sufficient. All of them maintained a solvency adequacy ratio of more than 150%, and no signs of systemic or regional risks were detected.

Protection Level Continued to Rise

In 2014, the non-life insurance industry's total sum insured was RMB 761.7 trillion Yuan, which was 12 times of nominal GDP, 13% up from a year earlier. The claim payment totaled RMB396.9 billion Yuan, 11.7% up from a year earlier. Insurance companies took an active part in disaster relief activities, giving full play to the insurance functions of improving and protecting people's livelihood and disaster relief, helping the affected districts quickly restore normal production and life. In 2014, the non-life insurance industry paid RMB 930 million Yuan to 1.187 million affected households in Liaoning Drought, paid RMB 1.55 billion Yuan and 420 million Yuan to Hainan, Guangdong and Guangxi hit by Typhoon Rammasun and Typhoon Kalmaegi respectively.

Life Insurance Market

Premium Income Grew Rapidly

In 2014, the life insurance market grew strongly, with premium income totaling RMB 1,268.73 billion Yuan, up by 18.2% YoY, 10.3 percentage points higher than 2013. As of the end of 2014, new policies premium income reached RMB 656.86 billion Yuan (+31.5% YoY), representing 51.8% of the total premium income of life insurance companies. Among these, the new installment payment policies contributed RMB 174.76 billion Yuan in premium (+18.9% YoY), accounting for 26.6% of the total premium of new life policies.

Product Structure was Remarkably Improved

Because of the market-oriented pricing reform of life insurance, the product structure was remarkably improved. In 2014, the premium income from ordinary life insurance stood at RMB 429.65 billion Yuan (+258% YoY), accounting for 33.9% of the total premium income of life insurance companies. Participating products premium income totaled RMB 650.88 billion Yuan (-20% YoY), representing 51.3% of the total premium income from life insurance companies. The premium income from unit-linked insurance reached RMB 440 million Yuan (+0.1% YoY), and the premium income from universal insurance reached RMB 9.19 billion Yuan (+5% YoY), representing 0.03% and 0.7% of the total premium from life insurance companies respectively.

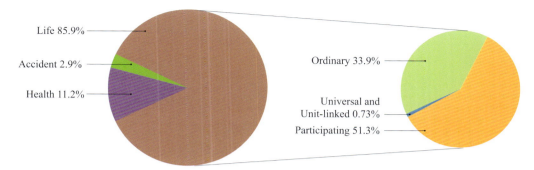

Chart 4   Portfolio of Life Insurance Business in 2014

In 2014, health insurance and accident insurance grew quickly. The premium income of health insurance totaled RMB 141.58 billion Yuan (+41.6% YoY), and accident insurance to totaled RMB 37.07 billion Yuan (+19.4% YoY). Together they accounted for 14.1% of the total life insurance premium, up by 1.8 percentage points from 2013.

Column 9   Official Implementation of the *Standard and Code of Disability Evaluation in Life Insurance*

On January 1,2014, the *Standard and Code of Disability Evaluation in Life Insurance* was officially implemented. The *Standard* further enlarged the protection coverage of accident insurance and improved the standardization of disability claim handling of accident insurance. The *Standard* also laid the foundation for future standardization, collection and analysis of accident insurance data, which could help the overall of upgrade the operation and management of accident insurance.

Steady Development of All Distribution Channels

In 2014, the individual agent distribution channel realized premium income of RMB 617.45 billion Yuan (+12.4% YoY), accounting for 48.6% of the total life insurance premium, 2.5 percentage points lower than the share in 2013. The bancassurance channel realized premium income of RMB 494.69 billion Yuan (+25.5% YoY), accounting for 39% of the total, 2.3 percentage points higher than 2013. Direct sales channel generated premium income of RMB 126.47 billion Yuan (+23.8% YoY), accounting for 10% of the total life premium income, 0.4 percentage points higher than 2013. Full-time institution agents contributed RMB 7.49 billion Yuan (-1.6% YoY). Part-time institution agents generated premium income RMB 16.34 billion Yuan (+3.6% YoY). Insurance brokers contributed RMB 6.28 billion Yuan (+38.9% YoY).

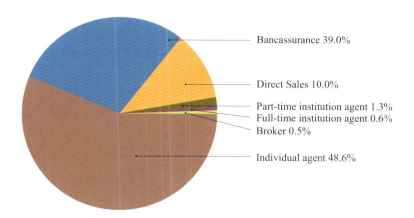

Chart 5   Distribution of Life Insurance Business in 2014

Industry Capacity Continued to Develop

As of the end of 2014, the total asset of life insurance companies amounted to RMB 8,254.54 billion Yuan (+20.8% YoY). The industry achieved net profits of RMB 109.27 billion Yuan, up by 119.6% from a year earlier. The solvency surplus increased significantly, further building up the capital buffer.

As of the end of 2014, there were 73 life insurance companies in the market, 3 more than that of 2013, among which 45 were domestic and 28 were foreign invested.

In 2014, the top 5 life insurance companies by premium income accounted for a combined market share of 62.4%, down by 7.1% percentage points YoY. This indicates further decline in market concentration.

Fast Growth of Compensation and Payout

In 2014, life insurance companies paid RMB 322.5 billion Yuan in compensation and payout(+21.6% YoY).

Table 2   Top 10 Life Insurance Companies by Premium Income in 2014

Rank	Name	Capital Structure	Premium (RMB billion Yuan)	Market share (%)
1	China Life Insurance Company Ltd.	Domestic	331.00	26.1
2	Ping An Life Insurance Company of China, Ltd.	Domestic	173.99	13.7
3	New China Life Insurance Co., Ltd.	Domestic	109.87	8.7
4	China Pacific Life Insurance Co., Ltd.	Domestic	98.69	7.8
5	PICC Life Insurance Company Limited	Domestic	78.63	6.2
6	Tai Kang Life Insurance Co., Ltd.	Domestic	67.90	5.3
7	Tai Ping Life Insurance Co., Ltd.	Domestic	65.13	5.1
8	Anbang Life Insurance Co., Ltd.	Domestic	52.89	4.2
9	Sino Life Insurance Co., Ltd.	Domestic	36.71	2.9
10	China Post Life Insurance Co., Ltd.	Domestic	21.95	1.7
	Total		1 036.77	81.7

Table 3   Claims Payment of Life Insurance Companies in 2014

Type	Claim Payment (RMB billion Yuan)	Growth rate YoY (%)	Share (%)
Life	270.48	20.2	83.9
Health	44.69	33.3	13.8
Accident	7.32	11.9	2.3
Total	322.49	21.6	100.0

Market Risks were Effectively Prevented

First, the maturity payment risk and the surrender risk were steadily resolved. In 2014, the surrendered premium value reached RMB 323.09 billion Yuan(+69.5% YoY), with the surrender ratio of 5.71%. The insurance industry constantly strengthened risk prevention, weathered the maturity payment and the surrender peak, and held the risk bottom line. Second, individual risks were successfully handled. The risk of individual companies was properly handled to maintain the stability of the whole industry. Thirdly, the life insurance industry maintained sufficient solvency. As of the end of the fourth quarter of 2014, only one life insurer was below the solvency standard, and the solvency ratio of other companies was above 150%. Fourth, the high cash value business developed in order. In the beginning of 2014, faced with the spurt of growth of the high cash value business, CIRC promptly adjusted its regulatory policies and released *Notice on Regulation of High Cash Value Insurance Products.* After the release of the *Notice*, the growth rate of the high value business declined by 80%, 85% and 84% in the second, third and fourth quarter respectively, and its precariously fast growth was effectively contained.

Insurance Intermediaries Market

Market Players

Full-time Institution Intermediaries

As of the end of 2014, there were 2,546 full-time institution intermediaries in China, 21 more compared with 2013. Out of the total number, there were 1,764 full-time insurance agencies, 445 insurance brokers and 337 loss adjusters. They had a registered capital of RMB 26.16 billion Yuan (+16.8% YoY).

Part-time Insurance Agencies

As of the end of 2014, there were 210,108 part-time agencies nationwide, including 179,061 from the financial sector, 31,047 from other sectors.

Performance of the Insurance Intermediaries Market

In 2014, insurance intermediaries contributed premium income totaling RMB 1,614.42 billion Yuan, accounting for 79.8% of the total insurance premium, 0.5 percentage point lower than that of 2013, including RMB 472.17 billion Yuan for non-life insurance and RMB 1,142.25 billion Yuan for life insurance.

Full-time Institution Intermediaries

In 2014, all full-time institution intermediaries achieved premium income of RMB 147.24 billion Yuan (+ 28.2% YoY), accounting for 7.3% of the total national premium income.

Insurance agencies produced a premium income of RMB 96.79 billion Yuan, accounting for 4.8% of the total national premium income, including RMB 89.3 billion Yuan for non-life insurance and RMB 7.49 billion Yuan for life insurance. Their commission income was RMB 18.48 billion Yuan, including RMB 15.66 billion Yuan of commission generated from non-life insurance and RMB 2.82 billion Yuan from life insurance.

Insurance brokers contributed RMB 50.45 billion Yuan of premium income, accounting for 2.5% of the total national premium income, including RMB 44.17 billion Yuan from non-life insurance, RMB 6.28 billion Yuan from life insurance. Insurance brokers generated a revenue of RMB 9.42 billion Yuan, including RMB 7.19 billion Yuan from non-life insurance, RMB 1.16 billion Yuan from life insurance, RMB 180 million Yuan from reinsurance and RMB 890 million Yuan as consulting fees.

Insurance loss adjusters' revenue was RMB 2.26 billion Yuan.

Part-time Agencies

In 2014, all the part-time agencies achieved premium income of RMB 700.89 billion Yuan, accounting for 34.6% of the total national premium income, including RMB 189.86 billion Yuan from non-life insurance, and RMB 511.03 billion Yuan from life insurance.

Individual Agents

In 2014, individual agents contributed premium income of RMB 766.29 billion Yuan, accounting for 37.9% of the total national premium income, including RMB 148.84 billion Yuan under non-life insurance and RMB 617.45 billion Yuan under life insurance.

Insurance Fund Investment

As of the end of 2014, the balance of insurance fund investment totaled RMB 9.3 trillion Yuan, accounting for 91.9% of the total assets of the industry, up by RMB 1.6 trillion Yuan or 21.4% from the beginning of the year.

Asset portfolio had several features. Firstly, fixed income products continued to be the main asset class, with debt investment such as government debt, financial debt and corporate debt standing at RMB 3.6 trillion Yuan, representing 38.2% of the total portfolio, and bank deposit at RMB 2.5 trillion Yuan, representing 27.1% of the total. Secondly, equity investment rose steadily, with the investment in stocks and mutual funds standing at RMB 1 trillion Yuan, representing 11.1% of the total investment, 1.1 percentage points higher than that of 2013. Thirdly, the alternative investment grew rapidly. The investment in long-duration equity shares was RMB 639.88 billion Yuan, accounting for 6.9% of the portfolio; the investment in real estate was RMB 78.44 billion Yuan, accounting for 0.8%; infrastructure investment plans amounted to RMB 731.7 billion Yuan, accounting for 7.8%. The above-mentioned 3 classes rose by 59%, 13.9% and 66% respectively compared with the beginning of the year.

Investment performance was good. In 2014, the whole industry realized investment return of RMB 535.88 billion Yuan, 170.05 billion more than in 2013. The financial return rate on investment was 6.3%, 1.3 percentage points higher than in 2013, and the overall return rate was 9.2%, 5.1 percentage points higher than in 2013. Both the financial and overall return rate broke the best records in the past five years.

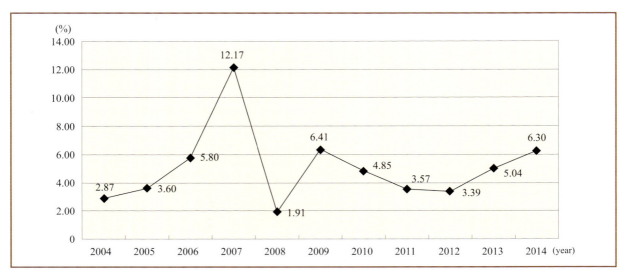

Chart 6   Investment Return from 2004 to 2014

Professional Reinsurance Market

Reinsurance Business Continued to Grow

In 2014, premium amounting to RMB 173.78 billion Yuan was ceded to reinsurers, 52% higher than that of 2013, among which RMB 92.94 billion (+7.7% YoY) were from non-life insurers, and RMB 80.84 billion Yuan (+188.6% YoY) were from life insurers. The rapid increase of the ceded life business was due to large scale of facultative reinsurance arrangements of some life insurers to ease their solvency pressure.

Reinsurance Companies Maintained Stable Growth

In 2014, reinsurers collected premium income of RMB 151.85 billion Yuan (+55.7% YoY) and made claim payment of RMB 39.3 billion Yuan (+11.2% YoY). They realized underwriting profit of RMB 1.17 billion Yuan and net profit of 5.88 billion Yuan.

Faster Expansion of Overseas Market

In 2014, premium of RMB settled cross-border reinsurance business reached RMB 9.54 billion Yuan, with 7 entities expanding to 4 markets namely, Hong Kong, Macao, Singapore and Chinese Taipei.

Reinsurance Capacity Increased Rapidly

As of the end of 2014, there were 1 reinsurance group company and 9 professional reinsurance companies. Supported by the *Opinions of the State Council on Accelerating the Development of Modern Insurance Service Industry* and C-ROSS, many large insurance companies intended to set up professional reinsurance companies, many off-shore reinsurers actively sought to set branches in the Chinese market, and social capital expressed great interest in the reinsurance market.

Opening up of the Chinese Insurance Market

Foreign-funded Insurance Companies in China

In 2014, the premium income of foreign-funded insurance companies reached RMB 90.19 billion Yuan (+32.6% YoY), accounting for 4.5% of the national total, up by 0.5 percentage point from that of 2013. Compensation and payout totaled RMB 47.2 billion Yuan. The total assets of foreign-funded insurance companies amounted to RMB 664.67 billion Yuan, up by 223.14 billion Yuan or 50.5% from the beginning of the year, accounting for 6.5% of the national total, 1.3 percentage points higher than 2013.

As of the end of 2014, insurance companies from 15 foreign jurisdictions had 56 foreign-funded insurance companies and established 140 representative offices in China.

Table 4 Growth of Foreign-funded Insurance Companies in Beijing, Shanghai, Guangzhou and Shenzhen in 2014

City	Premium income (RMB billion Yuan)	Growth (%)	Foreign-funded non-life insurance companies		Foreign-funded life insurance companies	
			Premium income (RMB billion Yuan)	Growth (%)	Premium income (RMB billion Yuan)	Growth (%)
Beijing	16.22	10.4	1.63	31.5	14.58	8.5
Shanghai	14.38	14.6	2.68	36.0	11.70	10.5
Guangzhou	10.53	29.6	1.33	17.7	9.22	31.7
Shenzhen	3.80	10.5	0.62	51.2	3.18	5.1

Foreign-funded Non-life Insurance Companies in China

In 2014, the premium income of foreign-funded non-life insurance companies totaled RMB 16.8 billion Yuan (+102.4% YoY), accounting for 2.2% of market share. The compensation payment of foreign-funded non-life insurance companies reached RMB 9.12 billion Yuan (+50.5% YoY).

In terms of business structure, auto, commercial property, liability, cargo, agriculture and accident insurance made up the major source of premium income of foreign-funded non-life insurers, accounting for 56.6%, 11.5%, 9.1%, 7.3%, 5.9% and 4.7% of the total respectively. The above mentioned six insurance lines altogether accounted for 95.1% of the total premium income of foreign-funded non-life insurance companies.

Table 5 Foreign-funded Non-life Insurance Companies by Premium Income

Rank	2014		2013		2012	
	Name	Market share in foreign-funded non-life insurance companies (%)	Name	Market share in foreign-funded non-life insurance companies (%)	Name	Market share in foreign-funded non-life insurance companies (%)
1	AXA Tianping	39.4	Groupama Avic	17.2	Chartis	16.4
2	Groupama Avic	8.7	AIG	13.8	Liberty Mutual	10.7
3	AIG	7.0	Liberty Mutual	10.2	Groupama	10.5
4	Starr	6.3	Allianz	7.9	Allianz	8.6
5	Allianz	5.3	Samsung	7.4	Samsung	7.7
	Total	66.7	Total	56.5	Total	53.9

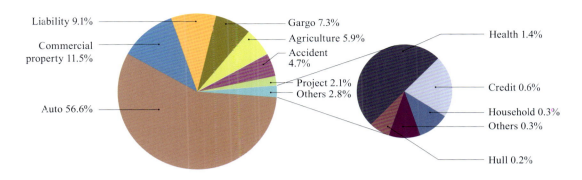

Chart 7   Foreign Non-life Insurance Business Mix

Foreign-funded Life Insurance Companies in China

In 2014, the premium income of foreign-funded life insurance companies totaled RMB 73.39 billion Yuan (+23% YoY), accounting for 5.8% of the total premium income of life insurance companies nationwide. The claim payment of foreign-funded life insurance companies reached RMB 13.69 billion Yuan (+60.2% YoY).

Table 6   Foreign-fundec Life Insurance Companies by Premium Income

Rank	2014		2013		2012	
	Name	Market share in foreign-funded non-life insurance companies (%)	Name	Market share in foreign-funded non-life insurance companies (%)	Name	Market share in foreign-funded non-life insurance companies (%)
1	ICBC-AXA Life	21.0	ICBC-AXA Life	17.2	AIA	18.3
2	AIA	14.4	AIA	15.8	ICBC-AXA Life	10.0
3	Met Life	9.2	Met Life	9.5	Met Life	9.8
4	Generali	7.6	Generali	8.0	Generali	8.8
5	Cigna-CMB	7.2	Cigna-CMB	7.1	CITIC-Prudential	7.6
	Total	59.4	Total	57.6	Total	54.5

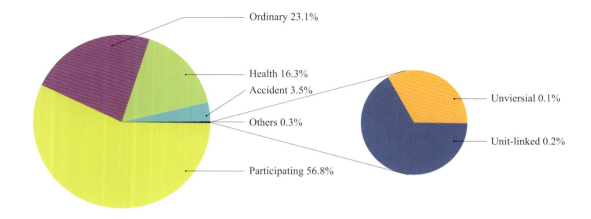

Ordinary 23.1%

Health 16.3%

Accident 3.5%

Others 0.3%

Participating 56.8%

Unviersial 0.1%

Unit-linked 0.2%

Chart 8   Foreign Life Insurance Business Mix

Foreign-funded Reinsurance Companies

Foreign-funded reinsurance companies collected premium income of RMB 98.35 billion Yuan (+104.1% YoY), accounting for 64.8% of the total reinsurance premium income across the country, and made claim payments of RMB 22.75 billion Yuan (+12% YoY). Total profit was RMB 1.82 billion Yuan (+72.8% YoY).

Overseas Operations of Chinese Insurance Companies

As of the end of 2014, 12 domestic insurers had set up 32 overseas operations, including 10 asset management companies. 4 domestic insurers had set up 7 overseas representative offices.

Photos by staff of the insurance industry

06

Reform and Innovation in Insurance Sector

- Insurance Industry Implemented the *Opinions* and Entered New Development Era
- Greater Market-orientedness Achieved through Comprehensive and Deeper Reform
- Insurance Market Became More Vigorous through Innovation and Development

Insurance Industry Implemented the *Opinions* and Entered New Development Era

In August 2014, the *Opinions of the State Council on Accelerating the Development of Mordern Insurance Service Industry (the Opinions)* was released. As a great mile stone for the development of modern insurance industry, the *Opinions* included 10 aspects, 32 items, with a clear theme, and proposed a series of powerful strategic measures for the reform and development of the insurance industry. The *Opinions* elevated the position of insurance industry. It defined the insurance industry as an important industry of modern economy for the first time, and gave a top-down design of how the growth of modern insurance service industry can be further boosted to play its part in the state governance system and governance modernization. The *Opinions* defined the strategic objectives. By 2020, insurance will be an essential means of risk management and financial management for government, enterprises and residents, with insurance penetration of 5% and insurance density of RMB 3,500 Yuan. To achieve this goal, the *Opinions* developed a comprehensive plan for the reform, development and regulation of insurance industry, and set clear requirement on improving insurance legal system to ensure the orderly development. The *Opinions* also upgraded supportive polices for the insurance industry including taxation incentives, fiscal and land use policies.

As an important strategic plan of the CPC Central Committee and State Council from the perspective of the overall social economic development, the *Opinions* provided guidance for insurance regulation under the new situation, and led the insurance industry to enter a new era of growth. The release of the *Opinions* caught a lot of attention at home and abroad. The international insurance community thought highly of the *Opinions*, acknowledged the leading position of China in realizing the function of insurance industry in social governance, and considered the *Opinions* an important contribution to international insurance development theory and practice.

Understanding and implementing the *Opinions* were the top priority of the insurance industry. CIRC developed the work plan for the implementation of the *Opinions,* held training seminars for CEOs of insurance companies, enhanced public awareness, and the leaders of CIRC gave lectures in provinces to promote the understanding of the *Opinions*. The Insurance Association of China, Insurance Society of China and CIRC branches organized training courses and seminars for the provincial offices of financial affairs and local governments. These governments worked out detailed plans for the *Opinions*. CIRC also worked closely with relevant central government departments in implementing the *Opinions*. A lot was achieved in implementing the *Opinions* in 2014.

First, market-oriented reform went deeper. CIRC set a framework of reform on universal insurance pricing mechanism based on research results and drafted the guidance of reform on commercial auto insurance pricing mechanism, and further promoted the reform on insurance fund investment. These market oriented reforms unleashed productivity and stimulated the market development.

Second, the market structure was further optimized. As of the end of 2014, there were 187 insurance institutions with 78,000 branches or subsidiaries nationwide. An open, balanced and vigorous modern insurance market system was basically formed with comprehensive, professional, regional insurance institutions and groups all developing, and captive insurance, mutual and internet insurers exploring new areas of growth.

Third, the insurance industry supported the social security system. It effectively filled the gap of social pension and health insurance through carrying out major illness insurance for rural and urban residents, managing medical protection plans, developing supplementary pension and health insurance, and managing corporate annuity plans and professional annuity plans, etc..

Fourth, the insurance industry actively supported modern agriculture. In 2014, the coverage of agriculture insurance continued to expand and the quality of service continued to improve. China is now the second largest agriculture market just after the Unit States, and the largest livestock insurance and forest insurance market.

Fifth, the insurance industry improved the disaster prevention and relief system as part of the social governance system. Liability insurance for food security, medical care and environment protection were encouraged to reduce disputes. CIRC also made explorations in catastrophe insurance system, pushed forward the legislation process of catastrophe insurance, and carried out pilot projects in this area.

Sixth, consumer interests were better protected. CIRC released *Opinions of CIRC on Strengthening Insurance Consumer Interest Protection* to address consumers' concerns. It also released *Notification of CIRC on Cleaning up the Unsettled Claims in 2014 and the Last 3 Years*, so that the public can better supervise work in this area.

In general, a good beginning was achieved for implementing the *Opinions* with a series of policies under development which would promote the long-term development of the industry, a number of reform measures in key area under promotion, and policy innovations emerging constantly. Government of all levels paid high attention: 21 provinces/ cities had already released documents to support the modern insurance service industry, 2 provinces/cities were about to do so, and 5 provinces/ cities had finished public consultation on the draft of the document.

The insurance industry is now standing at a new historic point, and will continue to serve economic and social development. To achieve that goal, and in accordance with the *Opinions*, market orientation and bottom-line thinking will persist to further unleash potential of the industry. It is foreseeable that with the support and guidance of the CPC Center Committee and State Council, and the hard work of the whole industry, the insurance industry will have an even brighter future.

Zhejiang Province Issued Implementation Details of the *Opinions*

On September 2, 2014, Zhejiang Provincial Government issued *Opinions about Further Enhancing the Role of the Insurance Industry in Promote the Development of Economy and Society,* becoming the first province issuing implementation details of the *Opinions*. This document put forward 10 solutions for promoting the development of insurance in Zhejiang, set 17 key government-industry cooperation projects including small loan guarantee insurance, catastrophe insurance, and designated related work to 19 departments of the provincial government. With the support of Provincial Office of Financial Affairs, Zhejiang Bureau held a meeting to work on the specific areas that insurance can help with economic and social development in Zhejiang. A province-level insurance think tank was established and field experience exchange meetings were held to encourage governments at all levels to enhance the role of insurers in social management or purchase insurance products and service so as to provide public services more efficiently. Zhejiang Bureau made efforts to expand the government-industry cooperation projects.

Column 10 Agricultural Target Price Insurance Proved to be Successful in Pilot Projects

In 2014, in accordance with the spirit of No.1 document of the central government and the *Opinions*, CIRC vigorously promoted target price insurance pilot projects and achieved good results. 20 provinces either launched the project or set out plans for it. Among them, Heilongjiang, Hebei, Henan and other 15 provinces had issued policies; Shandong, Liaoning and other 5 provinces had completed work plans, developed insurance products and planned to start in 2015. In 2014, 770,000 farmers participated in target price insurance. Premium income was RMB 280 million Yuan with risk coverage of RMB 6.2 billion Yuan (22 times as the premium income). The pilot projects provided target price insurance for crops, hogs, vegetables, and local featured agricultural products.

Column 11   Construction of Beijing Insurance Industrial Park Accelerated

On April 8, 2014, Beijing Insurance Industrial Park Innovative Development Seminar and the opening ceremony for the Industrial Park were held in Shijingshan District. The Chairman of CIRC, Mr. Xiang Junbo, Deputy Secretary General of Beijing Municipal Party Committee and Mayor Wang Anshun inaugurated the Industrial Park, giving their bless for the fast growth of the Industrial Park. The overall goal of the Industrial Park construction was to build a national financial show case led by the insurance industry. Its good environment and quality services will create a successful zone featuring experiment, industry clustering and advanced culture to attract insurance innovation.

Chinese Insurance Information Technology Company Inaugurated

On January 15, 2014, the Chinese Insurance Information Technology Company (CIITC) was formally established. The company was supposed to support the development of the industry, serve insurance regulation and protect customers by sharing information through a centrally managed, convenient, secure and efficient data sharing and interactive platform.

First Chinese Insurer Featuring Marine Insurance Started Business

On December 4, 2014, CNOIC received official approval from CIRC for business commencement. CNOIC was the first private national multi-line property insurer focusing on marine insurance and Internet business devoted to serving marine industries, coastal economy and coastal areas by providing comprehensive professional insurance services.

"New Directions, New Opportunities, New Future - Insurance Serving the Country"- Annual Academic Conference Held Successfully

On November 20 and 21, 2014, Insurance Society of China held the annual academic conference in Beijing with the theme "New Directions, New Opportunities, New Future - Insurance Serving the Country". In-depth discussions focusing on the *Opinions* were conducted. Chairman Xiang Junbo was present at the meeting and delivered an important speech. Mr. Li Yining, a famous economist, also attended the meeting and made a keynote speech about "New Normal and Insurance". The chairman of the International Insurance Society, Mr. Michael Morrissey, was invited to the meeting and spoke. The conference had a general meeting and 8 discussion panels. Over 800 representatives from departments of central and local governments and domestic and overseas insurers attended the conference.

Greater Market-orientedness Achieved through Comprehensive and Deeper Reform

Insurance Tariffs Reform Carried out Steadily

The Market-oriented Reform of Life Insurance Tariffs

Approved by the State Council, on August 5, 2013, CIRC launched a market-oriented reform of life insurance tariffs so as to establish a tariff formation mechanism in line with the socialist market economy. The reform started with ordinary products, then expanded to universal products, and will further include participating products. In 2013, the reform for ordinary life insurance was implemented, removing the upper limit of 2.5% on assumed interest rate, and prescribing reserves evaluation rate, and lowering capital requirements for protection products. In 2014, reform for universal insurance tariff was conducted on the basis of the experience of ordinary insurance tariff reform. Under the overall framework for life insurance tariff reform, CIRC revised the actuarial requirements for universal products. The detailed plan was thoroughly discussed and improved to achieve a better balanced relationship between innovation and risk control. As scheduled, CIRC would officially remove the ceiling on minimum guarantee interest rate of universal products in early 2015, and will try to lift the restriction on the assumed rate of participating products at the end of the year to realize full liberation.

Since the liberalization of assumed interest rate of ordinary life insurance, the policy was implemented smoothly and well received. Risks were under good control and the reform effect was obvious. First, there was sufficient product supply to meet the needs of the consumers. From the reform on August 5, 2013 to the end of 2014, 675 ordinary life insurance products with new rates were filed and approved, accounting for 23.4% of all the ordinary products filed at the same period. Secondly, prices went down. After the reform, the prices of mainstream ordinary products had dropped by 20% averagely, making customers more satisfied. Thirdly, business growth was fast. In 2014, the ordinary life insurance premium income reached RMB 429.65 billion Yuan, up by 258% year on year, accounting for 33.9% of the total life insurance premium income, 24 percentage points more than before reform, and became one of the growth engines for life insurance business. Fourthly, risks were effectively controlled. The whole industry had no spurts of surrenders or vicious competition and the transition from old products to new products was smooth.

The Reform of Auto Insurance Clauses and Tarrifs

In 2014, CIRC formally launched auto insurance clauses and tarrifs reform. First, CIRC clarified the overall framework of the reform. CIRC drew up *Opinions about Deepening the Reform on the Administration of Commercial Auto Insurance Clauses and Tariffs,* specified the overall goal, basic principles, main content and working schedule of the reform. Secondly, CIRC guided the Insurance Association of China in revising the model clauses and documents of auto insurance. In order to address most urgent concerns of the consumers, a national standard code for 160,000 different types of vehicles, giving each a unique "ID card" for the insurance industry. CIRC also studied assessment and protection mechanism for innovative clauses to improve their effectiveness and provide greater incentives for innovation. Thirdly, CIRC completed tariff measurement for the reform. The tariff measurement framework was designed to raise the accuracy of the calculation. CIRC organized multi-dimensional measurement on over 620 million pieces of auto insurance information and established the first auto insurance actuarial database. Multiple sets of tariff measurement solutions were designed to form a final report on auto insurance tariff reform. CIRC had finished the calculation for pure premiums, which is a major breakthrough in the reform.

The Reform of the Solvency Regulatory System

In 2014, CIRC successfully completed the design and review of 17 technical standards of the 3 pillars of C-ROSS. First, CIRC completed 9 regulatory rules of the first pillar on available capital, minimum capital, liabilities evaluation of life insurance policies, establishing risk-oriented quantitative capital measurement standards. Secondly, CIRC finished the design of rules for the second pillar on rating regulation (comprehensive risk rating), solvency risk management requirements and assessment, and rules for liquidity risk supervision. Thirdly, the technical standards for the third pillar were completed, establishing mechanisms for quarterly solvency disclosure, communication between regulator and stakeholders, and credit rating for insurers. Fourthly, CIRC completed rules for the insurance groups' solvency regulation, taking insurance conglomerates controlled by non insurance institutions under regulation for the first time and clarifying quantitative capital standards and solvency risk management requirements of insurance groups. Fifthly, CIRC developed the rules for solvency reporting, and established the solvency reporting system based on quarterly reports. Sixthly, according to the overall framework and technical standards of C-ROSS, revisions concerning related articles in the *Insurance Law* were also proposed.

Column 12   The Technical Framework of C-ROSS

C-ROSS is a three-pillar prudential supervision system based on China's insurance risk stratification model. The first pillar of quantitative regulatory requirements is aimed at addressing 3 kinds of quantifiable risks, namely, insurance risk, market risk and credit risk. It requires insurers holding capital reflecting those risk exposures. The second pillar of qualitative regulatory requirements is aimed at addressing operational risk, strategic risk, reputation risk and liquidity risk, which are difficult to quantify. This pillar evaluates the risk management competence of insurance companies. The market discipline mechanism of Pillar 3, through public information disclosure and transparency enhancement, leverages market disciplinary power to address risks which are difficult to address by the conventional regulatory tools of Pillars 1 and 2. C-ROSS is also a new framework for insurance group solvency regulation, taking insurance conglomerates controlled by non insurance institutions under regulation for the first time, thus able to supervise a series of complex risks.

Column 13   The Impact of C-ROSS

The design and implementation of C-ROSS was an important milestone in the history of China's industry development and regulatory reform, which will accelerate the modernization of China's insurance regulatory system, support the sustainable, fast and healthy development of the insurance industry, and have far-reaching impacts on the global insurance paradigm.

Firstly, it can facilitate the transformation of development mode. C-ROSS comprehensively measures all risks of insurers' business activities, strengthens solvency regulation on insurers, and guides insurers to balance risks and cost of capital in the pursuit of growth, so as they will abandon the extensive growth pattern for more efficient growth.

Secondly, it can promote risk management competence of the industry. C-ROSS established an incentive mechanism for risk management, regularly assessing risk management competence of insurers, taking risk management competence into the capital requirements and urging insurers to constantly improve their risk management to enhance the core competitiveness of their business.

Thirdly, it could make the industry more attractive to capital. C-ROSS releases capital, making capital use more efficient and thus increasing the insurance industry's attractiveness to social capital.

Fourthly, it can promote greater participation in international insurance cooperation and exchanges. C-ROSS was comparable to international mainstream regulatory regimes both in terms of the "three pillars" regulatory framework, and with regard to the specific aspects of regulatory standards and requirements, facilitating international exchanges and cooperation.

Market-oriented Reform of Insurance Fund Investment Going Deeper

In 2014, CIRC constantly deepened the reform of insurance fund investment, streamlining its procedures by releasing 12 policies to give more investment options and responsibility back to the market players themselves. A more dynamic and innovative market was the dividends of the reform. Firstly, CIRC steadily expanded the scope of investment. Insurance funds were allowed to be invested in Growth Enterprise Market stocks and inventory policies funds were allowed to be invested in blue-chip stocks, preferred stocks and venture capital funds, etc. Secondly, CIRC implemented a new multi-layered percentage regulation system based on insurance assets classes (not on breakdowns as the case before). Thirdly, CIRC deepened the reform of registration to improve the efficiency of product distribution. By the end of 2014, the product registration scale has reached RMB 1,064.437 billion Yuan. Compared with the previous size of 294.1 billion Yuan, registered funds' size over the past two years was 3.5 times of the seven years before. Fourthly, CIRC strengthened preventive regulation and damage control, focusing on information disclosure, internal control, supervisory rating, asset custody and recognition etc., forming a modern multi-level regulatory framework of "One Base, Five Instruments and Three Pillars".

Column 14   CIRC Promulgated *Notice about Strengthening and Improving Percentage Regulation on Insurance Funds*

In February 2014, CIRC issued *Notice about Strengthening and Improving Percentage Regulation on Insurance Funds*, which, on the basis of the regulations before, established a new percentage regulatory system based on insurance assets classes instead of on asset breakdowns as before. The new regulation is multi-leveled, differentiated and dynamic. The issuance and implementation of this *Notice*, integrated all rules on percentage regulation into one. On the one hand, the new rule greatly simplified the regulatory percentage requirements and preliminary realized international comparability; on the other hand, the new rule enhanced the vitality of the market, improved the efficiency of regulation, reflecting the regulatory philosophy of "liberalizing the front end and controlling the back end" and direction of regulation transformation.

Column 15   New Rules Concerning Insurance Fund Investment in 2014

◆ *Notice of CIRC about Insurance Funds Investing in Venture Capital*
◆ *Notice of CIRC General Office about Regional Supervision Pilot for Insurance Funds Investment*
◆ *Notice of CIRC and CBRC about the Standards of Insurance Asset Custody Business*
◆ *Notice of CIRC about the Trial Implementation of "Guidance for 5 Insurance Asset Risk Ratings"*
◆ *Notice of CIRC about Preferred Stocks Investment of Insurance Funds*
◆ *Notice of CIRC about Issuance of "Internal Control and Compliance Scoring Rules on Insurance Funds Investment"*
◆ *Notice of CIRC about Issuance of " Guidelines on Information Disclosure of Insurers' Fund Investment No. 1: Affiliated Transactions"*
◆ *Notice about the Insurance Investment in Trust Plans of Assembled Funds*
◆ *Notice about Authorization to Beijing Bureau and Some Other Bureaus to Carry out Pilot Supervision on Insurance Funds Investment*
◆ *Notice of CIRC about Standards of Bank Deposit of Insurance Funds*
◆ *Notice of CIRC about Strengthening and Improving Percentage Regulation on Insurance Funds*
◆ *Notice of CIRC about Insurance Funds Investing in GEM Stocks*

Column 16   The Establishment of Insurance Asset Management Association of China

On September 4, 2014, the founding conference of Insurance Asset Management Association of China and its first member congress were held in Beijing. The establishment of this association was one of the important achievements of market orientation reform and system innovation in the transformation of regulation approach. As the bridge linking market entities and regulators, the association will fulfill its functions of providing service to its members, protecting member interest, encouraging innovation and implementing industry self discipline. Its goal is to become a market-oriented, professional, modern and self-disciplined financial organization that reflects international experience so as to promote insurance asset management capability, lead innovation and encourage development of the industry.

Further Improving Market Access & Exit Rules

In 2014, CIRC, in accordance with the guiding philosophy of "liberalizing the front end and controlling the back end", further improved market access and exit mechanism, adhered to the market-orientation, highlighted the characteristics of specialization, balanced the relationships of development and regulation, regulation and service, investors' enthusiasm and consumers' benefits. CIRC combined market access with market structure upgrade considerations, improved market exit and resolution system, in order to facilitate an appropriate level of competition and a dynamic and vigorous market.

First, CIRC issued *Measures for Merger & Acquisition of Insurers* to provide various incentive policies and regulatory measures on M&A of insurers, gave full play to the crucial role of market mechanism. Secondly, CIRC continually improved the system for new insurers expanding business regions, encouraging them to focus on provincial insurance market for the first 2 years to accumulate experience. Thirdly, CIRC supported innovative entities, promoted the pilot initiative of professional online insurance company, expanded the pilot initiatives of captives and mutuals, showing support and encouragement to specialization and differentiation of the insurers' operating for better serving economic and social development. Fourthly, for better and more transparent market access reviewing, CIRC optimized the system of Domestic Market Access Reviewing Committee by completing its main responsibilities, auditing objects and organization structure, and adding committee members.

Column 17 *Measures for Merger & Acquisition of Insurers*

In March 2014, in order to further implement the spirit of the third plenary session of 18th CPC Central Committee and fully utilize the market mechanism to allocate insurance resources, regulate the behavior of the insurers' M&A, and promote the optimized allocation of insurance market resources, CIRC issued *Measures for Merger & Acquisition of Insurers*. It moderately expanded the sources of funding, relaxed shareholders' qualification requirements, and lifted the ban on horizontal acquisition. The *Measures* fully respected commercial wills, guided market self-discipline, stipulated regulatory measures including information disclosure, transition and lock-up period, and punishment mechanism.

Column 18 Internet Insurance Achieved Fast Development

In 2014, internet insurance grew with fast momentum in China. There were 94 insurers conducting internet insurance business, which contributed premium income of RMB 87.08 billion Yuan, which was 1.7 times compared to 2013. Internet insurance was sold by insurers directly on their e-commerce websites, through the websites of internet insurance brokers and agencies, on third party platforms, or by a professional Internet insurer. Internet insurance achieved very eye-catching growth throughout all the year as there were so many forms of conducting this business. For instance, on the 2014 "Double 11" Online Shopping Day, over 187 million policies of product return insurance was sold, a world record for the transactions amount of a single product line in a single day. The premium income of product return insurance was over RMB 100 million Yuan. Zhongan Online, a pilot professional Internet insurer, developed nearly 50 insurance products, achieved premium income of nearly RMB 800 million Yuan with insured amount totaling RMB 1.94 billion Yuan, and realized profits in its first year of business. On the regulation and supervision of internet insurance, CIRC both encouraged and watched the developments closely to make sure the development of internet insurance business was healthy and compliant with regulations. It drafted *Interim Measures for Internet Insurance Supervision,* holding consumer protection and risk prevention as priorities, setting out clear requirements on information disclosure, quality of service, data security, strengthening market exit regulation to control the risks.

Promoting Regulatory Reform of Insurance Products

The first was regulatory thinking upgrade. New rules were designed to strengthen product regulation. The focus was streamlining the regulatory procedure so as to give insurers greater freedom as well as more responsibilities. CIRC started the revision of *Measures for the P&C Insurance Companies' Clauses and Tariffs,* improving product regulation system and laying a solid foundation for the reform. It issued *Urgent Notice for Regulating Products Development and Sales of P&C Insurers* to regulate P&C insurance products' development, naming, selling and marketing, to better protect insurance consumers. The second was regulatory implementation improvement. CIRC started coding for life insurance products' terms, encouraged Insurance Association of China to establish a database and put it into use so that the public could scan QR codes or login the website of IAC to check the terms. A product information system was also established for more effective regulation. The third was other related work to consolidate product regulation. For example, CIRC guided IAC to promote easy-to-understand and standardized life insurance products and to revise its sample terms on the basis of international experience. It also guided the China Association of Actuaries in cash value research.

Improving the Status of Insurance Industry in the Auto Industry Chain

Insurance industry actively involved in the construction of post-automobile market system. In September 2014, CIRC and the Ministry of Transport, NDRC and other 6 ministries jointly issued *Guidance for Promoting the Transformation and Upgrading of Automobile Maintenance Sector and Improving Service Quality,* setting out a work plan for establishing a traceable system of auto parts to improving the environment for auto insurance business.

In 2014, under the guidance of CIRC, the Insurance Association of China cooperated with the China Association of Automobile Maintenance for the research and publication of "Parts to Whole Car" price ratio, so as to guide the idea of rational consumption and the correct understanding about vehicles' post-sale costs. This research released the ratio of the price of all auto parts to the price of the whole car as well as the ratio of the price of 50 fragile parts to the price of the whole car for 36 types of cars. The published research results led to a series of positive effects: the first was public recognition. After the ratios were published, they were viewed over 1 million times in the first 10 days. The second was the antitrust campaign in vehicle industry. The research for "Parts to Whole Car" ratio directly led to multiple investigations on vertical monopoly in vehicle industry by ministries such as NDRC. Thirdly, it had a positive role in curbing parts price soaring, letting consumers know their options of vehicle maintenance and repair, and improving the status of the insurance industry in the automotive industry chain.

Column 19   Characteristics of Domestic Vehicles' "Parts to Whole Car" Price Ratio

A research about the "Parts to Whole Car" price ratio of domestic common types of vehicles issued by the Insurance Association of China found: first, the ratio was generally high. Normally vehicles' "Parts to Whole Car" ratio was below 300% in foreign countries, but 30, or 83% of the 36 types of vehicles in this research had a ratio higher than 300%. Secondly, this ratio varied greatly among different vehicle types, with the highest ratio being 4 times higher than the lowest.

Insurance Market Became More Vigorous through Innovation and Development

In 2014, driven by reform and innovation, the insurance industry embraced new ideas and expanded their services. During explorations for new working mechanisms, this industry became more vigorous, provided more services and were more competitive.

Product Innovation

In 2014, insurance institutions focused on specialized and differentiated products. After studying the insurance needs carefully, they used their expertise to develop new products, which became new growth engines for their business as well as satisfied the needs of more consumers.

Sunshine P&C Launched Products for Unauthorized Charges to Protect Bank Account Safety

In 2014, Sunshine P&C Insurance formally launched "Sunshine Insurance for Unauthorized Charges", providing comprehensive protection for bankbooks, certificates of deposit, debit cards, credit cards (master and supplementary), online banking accounts, mobile phone bank accounts and third-party payment accounts so as to address the security issues of multiple accounts.

Funde Sino Launch Mobile Internet Annuity

In 2014, Funde Sino Life Insurance Company launched a mobile Internet annuity product called "baby piggy bank". Designed for children, this product was fun, easy to understand, personalized, convenient and flexible. Parents could put small money and change into the mobile phone piggy bank for their children.

Alltrust Insurance Succeed in Photovoltaic Power Plant Sunshine Index Insurance Program

In November 2014, Alltrust Insurance Company, in collaboration with SwissRe, successfully underwrote a sunshine index insurance program for 3 photovoltaic power plants. This insurance provided an effective transfer of power loss risk during the operation of the plant so as to ensure the estimated profits of the power stations, and meanwhile, helped raising credit for financing of the photovoltaic power programs.

Zheshang P&C Initiate Guarantee Insurance for Private Bonds

Zheshang P&C Insurance Company cooperated with Stocks Exchange Center of Zhejiang and Alibaba for carrying out guarantee insurance for private bonds. The innovative product provided financing guarantee of more than RMB 400 million Yuan for SMEs through its low-cost and transparent financing platform, helping them to get loans cheaper and faster.

China Continent Insurance Underwriting Liability Insurance for Blood Stations

In February 2014, Chongqing Branch of China Continent Insurance underwrote liability insurance for Chongqing blood station center, providing liability protection for the safe use of 300,000 bags of blood per year, mitigating the risk of disease and infection caused by blood transfusion. This product helped the blood stations to manage their blood more carefully and thus ensured public health security.

Service Innovation

In 2014, the insurance industry continued its innovation in services. Through mobile and internet technologies they raised the efficiency of underwriting, survey, loss adjustment and claims settlement. Customers were happy.

Guangdong Province: Better Service for Microfinance Guarantee Insurance

A SME Loan Guarantee Insurance Service Center in Jiangmen, Guangdong province was established in 2014. The service center was administrated by Insurance Association of Jiangmen and run by insurance companies with assistance from banks. It helped SMEs to get no-mortgage loans. The borrowing cost was made up of insurance premium and bank loan interest. It took only about 5 working days after the guarantee insurance policies were issued before the SMEs got the loans. The center was an initiative of insurance industry supporting the development of SMEs and serving local economic transformation and upgrading. It was a good example of what insurance industry could do for the SMEs with support from the government. The SMEs were very happy.

China Life's *Emergency Response Measures for Major Disasters*

To settle cases efficiently after major disasters hit, China Life worked out *Emergency Response Measures for Major Disasters*, which gave contingency plans, claims settlement standards, information disclosure procedures etc., based on the severity of the disaster. In the 19 major disasters including the missing Malaysia Airline MH370, earthquake in Yunnan Ludian, explosion in Jiangsu Kunshan and major auto accident in Tibet Nimu, China Life responded quickly and was widely praised by its customers.

Huatai Life Insurance Launched Telephone Service for Maturity Payment

In 2014, Huatai Life Insurance Company launched a telephone service for fast and convenient maturity payment. At the end of 2014, in the Shanghai branch which initiated the program, the percentage of telephone processing accounted for 57% of all maturity payment.

Tianan Property Insurance Launched An "Auto EasyPay" Mobile Video Survey System

Tianan Property Insurance launched an "Auto EasyPay" mobile video survey system in 2014 to connect customers, realizing real time video survey and synchronizing all the claiming processes including survey, adjustment, quotation, evaluation, checking and payment. The fastest record for the whole procedure was 16 minutes, much faster than before and more convenient for the customers.

Management Innovation

In 2014, insurance institutions continued improving their management mechanisms to raise operation efficiency, reduce cost and have stronger core competitiveness.

Fujian Policyholder Recording System Come into Running

In 2014, Fujian policyholder recording system came into running. The system could be downloaded into smart phones. Sales persons took photos of policy-holder signatures and their transcripts of risk warnings and then uploaded theses photos to a special platform. The system filled the gap of image collection in insurance sales, helped to improve the authenticity of insurance sales, contain practices such false signatures and transcriptions, laying a foundation for the use of big data.

Yantai Sub-bureau: Pay the Commission after Follow-up Call

In 2014, Yantai sub-bureau ruled that life insurers should not pay commissions for policies with duration of more than 1 year to party-time bank or postal agencies before making sure the customers expressed satisfaction in the follow-up calls. The purpose was to address problems as poor customer authenticity and low follow-up call rate, which were effectively relieved after the implementation of the rule. Consumer interest was better protected.

Changjiang P&C Insurance Used Procedure Manuals

Changjiang P&C Insurance used procedure manuals to better manage its business, control costs and risks. These are standardized and system procedures concerning reinsurance, compliance and legal affairs, inspection and auditing and customer service. These manuals achieved direct economic benefits of RMB 23.03 million Yuan for the company and significantly improved service efficiency, maintained compliance, and fostered a harmonious enterprise culture.

Institution and System Innovation

In 2014, the insurance industry sped up transformation of development pattern by strengthening operation management and business development through a series of comprehensive and deep reforms.

Beijing Implemented Differentiated Qualification Regulation on Insurance Sales Persons

In 2014, Beijing established differentiated qualification regulation on the sales persons, setting up different qualification standards for people selling participating products and universal insurance products, and for those selling unit-linked and variable annuities products. The sales persons of all life insurance companies and all full-time agencies selling life products in Beijing had to hold "Insurance Sales Qualification Certificate" and also pass relevant test. This rule will be formally implemented as of July 1ˢᵗ 2015. This rule will ensure that the sales persons are qualified people and will reduce misleading practices.

Taiping Life Open FTE Account for Cross-border Insurance Business

On August 21, 2014, Taiping Life Shanghai Free Trade Area branch opened a free trade account (FTE account), facilitating foreign currency denominated policy sales in China and RMB Yuan denominated policy sales in overseas market. Using the FTE account as a channel, Taiping conducted reinsurance ceding in and out and investment, to realize the two-way cross-border flowing of premiums in foreign and domestic currencies and maximize asset allocation efficiency.

Ping An Life Insurance Launched A Customer Manager System

In 2014, Ping An Life implemented an innovative system of customer manager, breaking the walls among internet selling, telephone selling and mobile selling, which greatly improved retention of customer managers and customer loyalty. Monthly fall-out rate of customer managers was 30% better than sales persons who are not customer managers.

Technology Innovation

In 2014, the insurance industry used internet-based big data, cloud computing, mobile communication to better analyze risk data and other related data and support innovation and development of the industry.

Auto Insurance Information Platform Realized Centralized Administration on National Level

In May of 2014, Chinese Insurance Information Technology Company (CIITC), successfully integrated regional auto insurance platforms to realize centralized administration on national level of the auto insurance information platform. It eliminated barriers to data sharing among different platforms before, realized the national wide auto insurance data collection and sharing. In the future, it would play an important role in pricing, tax collection, subrogation, and antifraud after system reconstruction and upgrading.

Jiangsu Became the First to Establish Information Sharing and Coordination Mechanism of Transportation and Insurance

In December 2014, Jiangsu Bureau and the provincial Public Security Department signed a strategic cooperation agreement on the establishment of an information sharing system that connects transportation management and insurance services to share data concerning motor vehicles, drivers, breaches of traffic rules, traffic accidents and basic auto insurance information. Through information sharing, the insurance industry had enhanced its risk identification and management.

CPIC Set up Mobile Application Laboratory

In June 2014, CPIC set up a mobile application laboratory. As an open mobile application R&D base and designed for new technology collection, tracking, research and development, incubation and test, this laboratory will become a place to experience the use of mobile applications in insurance and a place to promote the insurer's brand.

Anhua Agricultural Insurance Company Developed Implantable Electronic Tag Syringes

In 2014, Anhua Agricultural Insurance Company successfully developed the third generation of implantable electronic tag syringes, which can inject electronic tag with information such as about the underwriter, the insured time, and the I.D code into the pig's body so as to better identify the insured target. Death cause would also be written into the electronic tag and implanted in dead pigs so that they won't be sold in the market.

China Coal Insurance Company Drew and Issued Risk Map of Chinese Coal Mines

In October 2014, China Coal Insurance Company issued *Risk Map of Chinese Coal Mines*, which comprehensively assessed the safety conditions of all the coal mines national wide. The *Map* selected 5 indicators including gas levels, hydro-geological types, coal dust proneness to explosion, spontaneous combustion tendency of coal seam and pressure bumping, and took AHP method to establish the evaluation model. It rated the safety conditions by A, B, C and D. On the basis of safety assessment, in combination with the national coal mine safety quality standard system, taking into consideration human and non-human factors that could affect safety, a customer risk rating system was established so as to design underwriting schemes according to customer's risk rating, and providing targeted value-added services for coal enterprises such as risk prevention and disaster compensation.

Photos by staff of the insurance industry

Photos by staff of the insurance industry

07

Insurance Consumer Interest Protection and Consumer Education

- Top-level Design of the Insurance Consumer Interest Protection System
- Quick Dispute Resolution
- Addressing Insurance Consumers' Top Concerns
- Information Disclosure Related to Insurance Customers Stepped Up
- Consumer Education

Top-level Design of the Insurance Consumer Interest Protection System

In 2014, CIRC issued *Opinions of CIRC on Strengthening Insurance Consumer Interest Protection.* Reflecting the principles of IAIS on consumer protection and international experience and based on the actual situation of insurance consumer interest protection in China, this document clarified the guiding concept, basic principles and work objectives of insurance consumer interest protection, and raised the main tasks, direction as well as supporting measures. CIRC and NDRC jointly formulated *Construction Plan of China's Insurance Industry Credit System (2015-2020).* Based on the realities of China, this plan defined the goals and tasks of the insurance credit system construction in the next 5 years. It was China's first industry credit system construction plan, and also the guideline for the insurance industry in their fight to win confidence of consumers and society.

Quick Dispute Resolution

In 2014, CIRC strengthened the construction of 12378 insurance consumer complaints hotline, established 22 new hotline sub-centers in local bureaus, realizing full coverage of 12378 service network in all the bureaus. Through this hotline, local complaints can be dealt with locally and more quickly. By the end of 2014, the hotline received over 245,000 in-coming calls and achieved 98.5% of satisfaction.

In 2014, CIRC and its local bureaus received and processed 28,000 complaints. The number of disputes mediation organizations increased to 479 and more court suits were diverted to these institutions for mediation. Nearly 24,000 disputes were successfully settled in 2014. Closer cooperation with the Supreme People's Court to encourage disputes be settled at professional organization rather than in court proved to be productive. 139 cities with districts across the country now has this mechanism in place.

Addressing Insurance Consumers' Top Concerns

Firstly, CIRC continued to address reluctant payment of insurers. The result is that P&C insurers' average processing time (from reporting to finishing payment) for auto insurance claims with value amount below RMB 10 thousand Yuan was shortened from 90.4 days in 2012 to 21.2 days in 2014. Urged by CIRC to process their pending cases, P&C insurers cleared up 7.35 million pending property insurance claims, or 69.62% of all, paying RMB 95.1 billion Yuan for them in 2014. Secondly, the problem of misleading sales practices was tackled. Customers' information authenticity was strengthened and insurers were required to implement stricter supervision for misleading selling behaviors. CIRC also organized a specific taskforce to organize insurers to clear up their lapsed life insurance policies. 5.78 million lapsed life insurance policies that had been lapsed for no more than 2 years were cleared, involving cash value of RMB 22.94 billion Yuan with a clearing rate of more than 90%. Thirdly, CIRC reinforced investigation on activities harmful to consumers' benefits. CIRC conducted targeted inspections on insurers who the consumers complained a lot about to address the top concerns of the consumers. In 2014, CIRC local bureaus carried out 4601 on-site inspections, punished 156 institutions and 101 executives, gave fine tickets amounting to RMB 14.013 million Yuan, and conducted regulatory talks 348 times for consumer interest issues.

Information Disclosure Related to Insurance Customers Stepped Up

Firstly, CIRC released its regulatory administrative information concerning in accordance with the government's information disclosure requirements, including all insurance regulatory policies and regulations, administrative licensing results, administrative punishments, work in process and statistics and data through its official website. Secondly, CIRC regularly published information related to the interests of insurance consumers. CIRC released complaints data and key problems of insurers every quarter, publicized assessment of insurers' consumer complaints handling, clearing results of pending cases in P&C insurers and results of customer satisfaction survey for life insurers every year. In 2014, CIRC expanded information disclosure and disclosed to the public 5 typical cases of insurance consumers interest infringement. Thirdly, CIRC released risk warnings about the top complaints and the key concerns of insurance consumers regularly and irregularly through newspaper and internet to let the public be aware of the risks. In 2014, CIRC released 6500 insurance consumption risk warnings.

Consumer Education

Firstly, CIRC composed and published the first book series about insurance knowledge called "Xiao Bao Getting to Know Insurance", prefaced by CIRC Chairman Xiang Junbo and chief-editored by assistant Chairman Liang Tao. This book series were added into the purchase list of rural libraries by State Administration of Press, Publication, Radio, Film and Television. Secondly, CIRC used mobile platforms for insurance consumer education. Since the introduction of the official education WeChat account "regulator's classroom", for only 3 months subscribers had accumulated to over 7,000 at the end of 2014. Thirdly, CIRC created an education column in *Chinese Consumers News*, publishing 31 articles, which were also posted on www.ccn.com.cn. Fourthly, CIRC carried out insurance public education activities. On the "3·15" International Consumer Day and "7·8" National Insurance Day, nationwide publicity and education activities were organized including publishing articles, setting display boards, distributing pamphlets so as to let more people know about the functions, history and culture of insurance, and to promote rational consumption of insurance products.

Jiangxi Bureau Used "4 Third Parties" to Promote Consumer Interest Protection

Jiangxi Bureau used "4 third parties" to promote consumer interest protection: a third party review system of life insurance products, a third party assessment mechanism of auto insurance service quality, a third party mediation mechanism on insurance contract disputes and a third party testing center.

Mechanisms to Resolve Insurance Contract Lawsuits Through Mediation Covered Seen Everywhere in Henan

By setting up mediation rooms in courts, mediation centers or "insurance social courts" participated by mediation organizations and courts, the local insurance association of Henan Province created mechanisms to resolve insurance contract lawsuits through mediation in the 18 cities of Henan, resolving 1,885 disputes in this way in 2014.

Photos by staff of the insurance industry

08

Outlook of the Chinese Insurance Market in 2015

- A Promising External Environment
- A Promising Year for the Industry
- Another Year of Advancement for Insurance Regulation

A Promising External Environment

Experiencing profound changes in economic structure, development driving forces and market mechanism, against the backdrop of a shifting international environment, China's macro economy is now in a new stage of development. In this new situation of the economy, the CPC Central Committee and the State Council made visionary decisions to deepen reform, streamline administration and delegate power to the lower levels. Meanwhile, series of innovative developing strategies including One Belt One Road and new urbanization are implemented to facilitate the transformation and upgrading of economic and industrial structure. This gives many opportunities for the insurance industry to further expand its services, improve its service quality and play a bigger role in social management.

A Promising Year for the Industry

As the development policy of the insurance sector gradually shows its effect, and the Party's Central Committee and State Council are seeking to improve the governance of the country and modernize its governance capability, as people become more and more aware of risks and insurance, the insurance industry enjoys a favorable environment for further development. The issuance of the *Opinions* demonstrates that it is now the government's will to developing insurance. The role of insurance has been uplifted to the national governance level, which implies insurance will become one of people's living necessities. For this underinsured country with large population and GDP, the next 5 to 10 years will be a golden period for the development of insurance industry. We are fully entitled to believe that the insurance industry will maintain the momentum of steady, rapid and profitable growth and deliver more benefits to the society in 2015.

Another Year of Advancement for Insurance Regulation

In 2015, fully implementing the principles of the Party's 18th Congress and its third and fourth plenary sessions, the Central Economic Working Conference, and the series of important speeches of Party General Secretary Xi Jinping, CIRC will seek progress while maintaining stability, adapt to the economic "new normal" and implement the *Opinions* in detail. It will continue to focus on better services, strict supervision, risk prevention and development, advance the transformation and upgrading of the insurance industry for better development quality and efficiency so as to foster a market that is not only big but also strong. This will be anchored on reform and innovation, implementation of policies, risk prevention and consumer protection.

09

Appendices

Appendix 1   Important Regulatory Trends of the Chinese Insurance Market in 2014

On January 8, the CIRC and the China Banking Regulatory Commission jointly released the *Notice on Further Strengthening Regulation on Commercial Banks Selling Insurance*, effective as of April 1, 2014. The *Notice* further strengthens the regulation of Bancassurance requirements on target buyers and product structure.

On January 15, Chinese Insurance Information Technology Co., Ltd. was founded to provide IT support and service to Chinese insurance market and regulation.

On January 21, the 2014 National Insurance Regulatory Conference was held in Beijing. Mr. Xiang Junbo, Secretary of the CPC committee, Chairman of the CIRC attended the conference and gave the keynote speech.

On February 19, the CIRC released the *Notice on Strengthening and Improving Percentage Regulation of Insurance Asset Management,* in order to establish a multi-layered, differentiated and dynamic proportion regulation system based on asset classification.

On February 21, the 9th Sino-US Insurance Dialogue and the Sino-US Insurance Regulation Seminar between the CIRC, the Office of the United States Trade Representative and NAIC were held in Fuzhou.

On February 28, the CIRC released the *Notice on Regulation of Bank Deposits of Insurance Assets*, to strengthen the review of qualification of the counterparty, set up a custody mechanism, supervise the pledge of deposit, and enhance reporting requirement.

On March 8, the CIRC released *Emergency Notice on Dealing with the Missing MH 370 Flight*, to urge the insurance industry to react to the accident properly.

On March 21, the CIRC released the *Administrative Measures on Merger and Acquisition of Insurance Companies*, to moderately ease the criteria of fund source and shareholder qualification, allow insurance companies to purchase another insurance company, and provide for stricter information disclosure, acquisition transition period and punishment to violation.

On March 25, the CIRC released *Guidance on Insurance Industry Serving the Development of New Urbanization*, which set six key measures to support new urbanization, such as exploring roles of insurance industry in the new urbanization development, gradually turning insurance industry to an important pillar of the multi-layered urban-rural social security system, an important financing channel of urbanization, and an important tool to improve society management and public service, and an effective way to deal with catastrophes.

On April 2, the CIRC released *Notice on Authorizing CIRC Beijing Bureau and Other Bureaus to Regulate Insurance Asset Management*, to delegate certain regulatory power over insurance fund management to six CIRC Bureaus in order to set up a multi-layered insurance fund management regulatory system.

On April 24, the PBC, CBRC, CSRC, CIRC and SAFE jointly released *Notice on Regulation of Inter-finance Business*, which raised 18 requirements in the operation of inter-finance business, internal and external management, and innovation of asset-liability business, to push forward adjustment and transformation of economic structure.

On May 15, the General Office of the CIRC released *Notice on Further Simplifying Administrative Examination and Approval Procedure to Support China (Shanghai) Free Trade Zone*, allowing a pilot project of institute clause for marine insurance, canceling approval requirement for some insurance companies in setting branches and appointing senior executives.

On June 17, the CIRC released *Guidance on Pilot Reversed Mortgage Pension Insurance*, to encourage insurance industry to actively participate in aging-care service and explore new ways in improving old-age protection system.

On July 5, Beijing Insurance Research Institute was founded, to conduct research on strategic issues of the Chinese insurance market and social economy and major policy measures of insurance regulation, striving to become an insurance intellectual platform and talent base.

On July 8, the 2014 National Insurance Publicity Day was held in Beijing, in which the first issue of *White Paper on Social Responsibility of China's Insurance Industry* was released. Mr. Xiang Junbo, Chairman of the CIRC, and Mr. Li Yang, Vice President of the Chinese Academy of Social Sciences, attended the activity and gave speeches.

From July 17 to 18, the ninth Asian Forum of Insurance Regulators (AFIR) was held in Beijing. Mr. Xiang Junbo, Chairman of the CIRC was elected Chairman of AFIR.

On July 28, the CIRC and Zhejiang Province Government jointly released *Notice on Establishing Insurance Innovation and Show Case Zone in Ningbo City Zhejiang Province*, to explore sustainable insurance reform and innovation that can be copied and promoted.

On August 10, the State Council released *Opinions on Accelerating the Development of Modern Insurance Service Industry*. As a blue print for the insurance industry in a certain period to come, it gave insurance industry a critical role in the strategic plan of social economic development, set the strategic development targets, and set out a plan to expand insurance services, provide more supportive policies and deepening reform and opening up.

On September 4, the founding conference and first representative meeting of the Insurance Asset Management Association of China was held in Beijing. Mr.Xiang Junbo, Chairman of the CIRC attended the meeting and gave a speech.

On September 28, the CIRC released *Interim Measures on Regulation of Non-insurance Subsidiaries of Insurance Companies*, to enhance risk monitoring and prevent risk transfer with indirect regulation, in order to protect insurance consumers' interest and promote the sound development of the insurance industry.

On October 17, the CIRC released *Notice on Insurance Fund Investing in Preferred Stocks*, to further broaden investment channel of insurance funds, optimize asset allocation, and prevent investment risks.

On October 17, the CIRC released *Guidance on Insurance Asset Classification,* to guide insurance companies to strengthen asset risk management and improve the efficiency and quality of asset management.

On November 13, the CIRC released *Solvency Reporting Standard No. X: Solvency Report (for consultation)*, to solicited public opinions. All the 17 rules of C-ROSS technical standards were for public consultation.

On November 14, the CIRC released *Opinions on Strengthening the Protection of Insurance Consumers' Interests*. It was the first policy document issued by a financial regulator to set comprehensive and detailed guidance on consumer protection for the whole industry.

On November 17, the State Council released *Opinions on Accelerating the Development of Commercial Health Insurance*. For the first time, the central government defined the role of commercial health insurance in deepening medical and health care system reform, developing health care industry and promoting the transform and upgrade of economy. It was the first document dedicated to the development of commercial health insurance.

On November 21, the founding conference of China Agriculture Insurance Reinsurance Pool was held in Beijing. The Pool was founded by 23 insurers licensed to conduct agriculture insurance and one reinsurer, to pool resources and improve the risk management of agriculture insurance.

On December 2, the CIRC and Guangxi Zhuang Autonomous Region Government signed an MOU in Nanning, to conduct deep cooperation in creating good environment for insurance industry development, improving insurance market system and increasing insurance fund investment. By then, the CIRC had signed MOU with 18 provinces (autonomous regions or municipal cities) and municipalities with independent planning status.

On December 4, the CIRC released *Guidance on Consolidated Regulation of Insurance Groups*, to monitor risks from group wide perspective and prevent financial risk transfer.

On December 12, the CIRC released *Notice on Insurance Fund Investing in Venture Capital Fund*, to regulate insurance fund investing in venture capital fund, support the sound development of start-ups and micro enterprises, and prevent investment risks.

On December 15, the CIRC released *Notice on Carrying out Inspection in Insurance Companies on "Two Strengthens, Two Curbs"*, to identify the outstanding problems and risks in insurance company's governance through the inspection, solve the problems accordingly, and establish a long-term mechanism in preventing and solving risks.

On December 18, the CIRC, Office of the Commissioner of Insurance of Hong Kong and Monetary Authority of Macao signed the cooperation agreement in Macao to fight against insurance fraud together.

On December 26, the second meeting of the Cross-Strait Insurance Regulatory Cooperation Mechanism was held in Beijing. Based on previous agreement, this meeting further discussed deepening cross-strait insurance regulatory cooperation.

On December 30, the CIRC released *Guidance for Insurance Institutes on Risk Assessment and Client Classification of Money Laundering and Terrorist Financing*, to guide insurance institutes in assessing risks of money laundering and terrorist financing, set appropriate money laundering risk levels of client, and improve the efficiency of anti-money laundering and anti-terrorist financing.

Photos by staff of the insurance industry

Appendix 2 Main Insurance Indicators of China during 2004—2014

Table 1 Distribution of Premium Income, 2004—2014[1]

Year	Insurance Premium		Life Insurance		Non-life Insurance	
	Total Amount (RMB 100 million)	Growth Rate (%)	Total Amount (RMB 100 million)	Growth Rate (%)	Total Amount (RMB 100 million)	Growth Rate (%)
2004	4,323.0	12.3	3,198.2	7.20	1,124.8	30.0
2005	4,928.4	14.0	3,644.9	14.00	1,283.1	14.1
2006	5,640.2	14.4	4,059.1	11.3	1,581.1	23.2
2007	7,033.4	25.0	4,946.5	21.9	2,086.6	32.0
2008	9,789.1	39.2	7,342.6	48.5	2,446.2	17.3
2009	11,137.3	13.8	8,144.2	11.0	2,992.9	22.4
2010	14,528.0	30.4	10,500.9	28.9	4,026.9	34.6
2011	14,341.0	10.5	9,560.0	6.9	4,780.9	18.7
2012	15,485.5	8.0	9,955.4	4.1	5,530.1	15.7
2013	17,217.9	11.2	10,736.5	7.9	6,481.2	17.2
2014	20,233.6	17.5	12,687.3	18.2	7,546.1	16.4

Table 2 Insurance Penetration and Insurance Density, 2004—2014[2]

Year	Insurance penetration (%)	Insurance density (RMB per person)
2004	3.39	332.2
2005	2.70	375.6
2006	2.80	431.3
2007	2.93	532.4
2008	3.25	736.7
2009	3.32	834.4
2010	3.65	1,083.4
2011	3.04	1,064.4
2012	2.98	1,143.7
2013	3.03	1,265.4
2014	3.18	1,479.3

Table 3 Insurance Fund Investment Return, 2004—2014

Year	Investment Return (%)
2004	2.87
2005	3.60
2006	5.80
2007	12.17
2008	1.91
2009	6.41
2010	4.85
2011	3.57
2012	3.39
2013	5.04
2014[3]	6.30

[1] The premium income from 2004 to 2010 was statistical data prior to the implementation of *Interpretation No. 2 of the Accounting Standards for Business Enterprises*.

[2] The insurance penetration and the insurance density from 2004 to 2010 are calculated according to the data prior to the implementation of *Interpretation No.2 of the Accounting Standards for Business Enterprises*.

[3] Data are taken from the website of the National Bureau of Statistics, where 2014 GDP RMB 63.6463 trillion Yuan, total population as of end 2014 at 1.36782 billion.

Table 4   Distribution of Premium Income by Region, 2014

Region	Direct Insurance Premium Income			Property & Casualty Insurance			Personal Insurance		
	Accumulative (RMB100 million)	YoY Growth (%)	Proportion (%)	Accumulative (RMB100 million)	YoY Growth (%)	Proportion (%)	Accumulative (RMB100 million)	YoY Growth (%)	Proportion (%)
National Total	20,233.6	17.5	100.0	7,203.5	16.0	100.0	13,030.1	18.4	100.0
1. Independent Business Income of Headquarters	96.8	13.6	0.5	94.6	13.5	1.3	2.2	6.5	0.0
2. East Region	11,709.0	17.8	57.9	4,139.6	15.4	57.5	7,569.4	19.2	58.1
Beijing	1,207.3	21.3	6.0	314.8	9.3	4.4	892.5	26.2	6.9
Tianjin	317.7	14.8	1.6	108.9	6.5	1.5	208.9	19.7	1.6
Hebei	931.9	11.2	4.6	356.7	15.2	5.0	575.2	8.9	4.4
Liaoning	558.0	25	2.8	187.4	13.3	2.6	370.6	32.0	2.8
Dalian	199.3	13.2	1.0	71.9	13.0	1.0	127.4	13.4	1.0
Shanghai	986.8	20.1	4.9	320.4	12.3	4.5	666.4	24.3	5.1
Jiangsu	1,683.8	16.4	8.3	606.3	16.9	8.4	1,077.5	16.2	8.3
Zhejiang	1,051.1	13.8	5.2	472.9	13.9	6.6	578.2	13.7	4.4
Ningbo	207.0	11.6	1.0	111.6	15.2	1.6	95.4	7.6	0.7
Fujian	554.7	19.8	2.7	182.2	15.9	2.5	372.5	21.8	2.9
Xiamen	131.2	17.4	0.7	57.1	18.6	0.8	74.1	16.5	0.6
Shandong	1,250.3	13.5	6.2	426.5	15.1	5.9	823.8	12.7	6.3
Qingdao	203.1	13.6	1.0	88.1	17.3	1.2	115.0	10.9	0.9
Guangdong	1,792.8	25.0	8.9	590.1	21.1	8.2	1,202.7	27.0	9.2
Shenzhen	548.7	17.1	2.7	207.0	19.8	2.9	341.7	15.5	2.6
Hainan	85.1	17.3	0.4	37.8	19.3	0.5	47.3	15.7	0.4
3. Middle Region	4,598.9	18.7	22.7	1,460.1	16.5	20.3	3,138.8	19.8	24.1
Shanxi	465.4	12.9	2.3	156.0	7.9	2.2	309.3	15.5	2.4
Jilin	330.0	25.1	1.6	107.7	18.2	1.5	222.3	28.8	1.7
Heilongjiang	507.1	31.9	2.5	122.0	7.4	1.7	385.1	42.3	3.0
Anhui	572.5	18.6	2.8	241.4	18.5	3.4	331.0	18.6	2.5
Jiangxi	400.2	25.9	2.0	138.7	19.4	1.9	261.5	29.7	2.0
Henan	1,035.6	13.0	5.1	278.4	16.6	3.9	757.2	11.8	5.8
Hubei	700.1	19.2	3.5	204.6	20.8	2.8	495.5	18.5	3.8
Hunan	588.0	15.7	2.9	211.3	20.0	2.9	376.8	13.4	2.9
4. West Region	3,828.9	15.4	18.9	1,509.2	17.2	21.0	2,319.7	14.2	17.8
Chongqing	407.0	13.7	2.0	138.9	23.4	1.9	268.1	9.2	2.1
Sichuan	1,060.8	16.0	5.2	371.8	18.0	5.2	689.0	14.9	5.3
Guizhou	212.2	16.8	1.1	112.4	26.3	1.6	99.8	7.7	0.8
Yunnan	376.1	17.3	1.9	177.3	16.8	2.5	198.8	17.7	1.5
Tibet	12.8	11.6	0.1	9.0	13.2	0.1	3.7	7.9	0.0
Shaanxi	476.9	14.3	2.4	160.0	16.7	2.2	316.9	13.1	2.4
Gansu	208.4	15.7	1.0	80.0	17.1	1.1	128.4	14.9	1.0
Qinghai	46.0	17.9	0.2	23.0	17.9	0.3	23.0	18.0	0.2
Ningxia	83.9	15.4	0.4	36.4	15.8	0.5	47.5	15.1	0.4
Xinjiang	317.4	16.1	1.6	131.6	16.3	1.8	185.8	15.9	1.4
Inner Mongolia	314.0	14.3	1.6	138.3	6.6	1.9	175.8	21.3	1.4
Guangxi	313.3	13.7	1.6	130.6	16.5	1.8	182.7	11.9	1.4

Table 5   2014 Balance Sheet of the Chinese Insurance Industry

Unit: RMB100 million

Assets	Beginning of the year	End of the year	Total Equity and Liabilities	Opening Balance	Ending Balance
Assets:			**Liabilities:**		
Cash	2,641.0	3,453.4	Short-term borrowings	55.5	100.0
Lending funds	0.7	0.7	Guarantee deposits received	82.4	546.9
Financial assets at fair value through income	1,634.0	2,142.3	Borrowing funds	25.0	0.0
Derivative financial assets	0.3	0.2	Financial liabilities at fair value through income	0.7	100.9
Financial assets purchased under agreement to resell	838.2	754.9	Derivative financial liabilities	0.1	0.7
Interest receivable	1,224.7	1,521.7	Assets sold under agreements torepurchase	3,650.5	4,271.4
Premium receivable	580.0	723.6	Brokerageand commission expensespayable	176.5	225.6
Assets management fee receivable	12.1	18.0	Commission expenses payable for pension	0.0	0.0
Pension management fee receivable	3.3	6.6	Premiums received in advance	492.7	827.9
Subrogation receivable	41.5	40.8	Salaries and employees' welfare payable	325.9	466.7
Reinsurance receivable	764.3	681.9	Taxes payable	139.9	268.2
Reinsurance unearned premium reserve receivable	393.0	357.7	Insurance Security Fund	29.4	34.3
Reinsurance outstanding claims reserve receivable	562.8	613.4	Claims payable	951.9	1,149.6
Reinsurance life reserves receivable	347.0	1,320.3	Other payables	487.0	714.7
Reinsurance long-term health reserves receivable	94.7	103.5	Policyholder dividend payable	1,268.2	1,647.8
Policy loans	1,335.1	1,800.9	Reinsurance payable	910.4	1,430.9
Loans	5,526.5	9,297.7	Unearned premium reserves	3,325.5	3,793.9
Guarantee deposits	230.0	827.6	Outstanding claims' reserves	3,035.3	3,537.3
Term deposits	18,823.0	20,201.0	Including: IBNR	764.2	993.6
Available-for-sale financial assets	17,889.7	23,120.2	Life insurance reserves	44,428.1	50,501.4
Hold-to-maturity investment	21,203.4	22,339.9	Long-term health insurance reserves	1,869.9	2,235.7
Long-term equity investments	3,989.8	6,034.0	Policyholders' deposits	9,591.5	12,237.0
Statutory deposit	926.1	1,111.2	Long-term borrowings	52.2	20.7
Investment properties	732.4	824.4	Bonds payable	2,301.8	2,391.0
Fixed assets	769.1	811.1	Fund of satellite insurance	1.8	1.8
Intangible assets	272.4	298.7	Independent account liabilities	823.3	1,096.4
Independent account assets	823.3	1,097.6	Deferred income tax liabilities	119.2	399.9
Deferred income tax assets	212.0	89.2	Current accounts within group (Credit)	54.6	86.9

Continued

Assets	Beginning of the year	End of the year	Total Equity and Liabilities	Opening Balance	Ending Balance
Current accounts within group (Debit)	61.8	80.3	Internal current accounts (Credit)	65.2	88.2
Internal current accounts (Debit)	64.4	85.9	Other liabilities	186.5	298.4
Other assets	1,042.2	1,805.9	Total liabilities	74,450.9	88,474.8
			Owners' Equity:		
			Paid-in capital	3,721.0	4,308.0
			Capital reserves	2,313.0	4,406.4
			Less: Treasury share	0.0	0.0
			Surplus reserves	174.1	240.6
			Generic Risk Reserve	81.0	514.6
			Retained earnings	1,333.1	2,293.6
			Foreign translation gain or loss	(0.8)	0.2
			Minority equity	966.7	1,326.2
			Total Owners' Equity	8,588.0	13,089.6
Total Assets	83,038.9	101,564.4	Total Liabilities and Owners' Equity	83,038.9	101,564.4

2015中国保险市场年报

ANNUAL REPORT OF THE CHINESE INSURANCE MARKET 2015

责任编辑：肖丽敏
责任校对：李俊英
责任印制：裴　刚

图书在版编目（CIP）数据

2015中国保险市场年报（2015 Zhongguo Baoxian Shichang Nianbao）/中国保险监督管理委员会编. —北京：中国金融出版社，2015.6

ISBN 978 – 7 – 5049 – 8011 – 3

Ⅰ.①2…　Ⅱ.①中…　Ⅲ.①保险市场—研究报告—中国—2015　Ⅳ.①F842.6

中国版本图书馆CIP数据核字（2015）第131770号

出版
发行　**中国金融出版社**

社址　北京市丰台区益泽路2号
市场开发部　（010）63266347，63805472，63439533（传真）
网上书店　http://www.chinafph.com
　　　　　（010）63286832，63365686（传真）
读者服务部　（010）66070833，62568380
邮编　100071
经销　新华书店
印刷　北京侨友印刷有限公司
装订　平阳装订厂
尺寸　210毫米×296毫米
印张　9.75
字数　240千
版次　2015年6月第1版
印次　2015年6月第1次印刷
定价　130.00元
ISBN 978 – 7 – 5049 – 8011 – 3/F.7571
如出现印装错误本社负责调换　联系电话（010）63263947

国务院发布保险业"新国十条"

保险 让生活更美好

保险是现代经济的重要产业和风险管理的基本手段，是社会文明水平、经济发达程度、社会治理能力的重要标志。

建设有市场竞争力，富有创造力和充满活力的现代保险服务业，使现代保险服务业成为完善金融体系的支柱力量，改善民生保障的有力支撑、创新社会管理的有效机制、促进经济提质增效升级的高效引擎和转变政府职能的重要抓手。

到2020年，基本建成与我国经济社会发展需求相适应的现代保险服务业，努力由保险大国向保险强国转变，保险深度达到5%，保险密度达到3 500元/人，保险的社会"稳定器"和经济"助推器"作用得到有效发挥。

保险系统员工摄影作品

目录

主席致辞

　　2014年是保险业具有历史性意义的一年。8月，国务院发布了《关于加快发展现代保险服务业的若干意见》，对新时期保险业改革、发展和监管进行了全面部署，提出了加快建设世界保险强国的战略目标。10月，国务院办公厅出台了《关于加快发展商业健康保险的若干意见》，第一次从深化医药卫生体制改革、发展健康服务业、促进经济提质增效升级的高度，定位商业健康保险的功能作用。这两个重要文件的出台，翻开了中国保险业加快发展和走向腾飞的新篇章，在中国保险业发展史上具有里程碑意义。

　　一年来，在党中央、国务院的正确领导下，保险业在复杂困难的形势下，坚持抓服务、严监管、防风险、促发展，各项工作扎实推进，改革发展实现了重大跨越。面向未来，保险业已经站在新的发展起点上。

行业实现快速发展

　　面对增长速度换挡期、结构调整阵痛期和前期刺激政策消化期"三期叠加"的挑战，中国保监会简政放权，推动行业持续深化改革，在宏观经济下行的背景下驶入了发展的快车道。从业务增速来看，2014年全国保费收入突破2万亿元①大关，增速达到17.5%，是国际金融危机以来最高的一年。其中，财产险保费收入7 203.5亿元，同比增长16%；人身险保费收入1.3万亿元，同比增长18.4%。从业务结构来看，结构调整走向深入，与实体经济联系紧密的保证保险同比增长66.1%，与民生保障关系密切的年金保险同比增长77.2%，保障性较强的健康保险同比

---

① 除特殊说明外，本年报中数据为执行《企业会计准则解释第2号》后的年度审计数据。

增长41.9%。从经营效益来看，保险公司实现利润总额1 934.2亿元，同比增长91.4%，保险资金运用实现收益5 358.8亿元，同比增长46.5%，创历史新高。保险资金投资收益率达6.3%，同比提高1.3个百分点，创五年来最好水平。

改革创新不断深化

一年来，中国保监会把全面深化改革作为带领保险业走出困境的突破口，全年改革亮点纷呈。保险费率形成机制改革稳步推进，万能保险费率市场化改革方案和商业车险条款费率管理制度改革方案已报国务院，在发挥市场配置资源的决定性作用方面又迈进了一大步。市场准入退出制度改革进一步完善，创新发展自保、相互、互联网等新型市场主体。保险资金运用改革不断深化，配置多元化格局基本形成，资金运用风险总体可控。巨灾保险制度建设取得积极进展，制订巨灾保险制度方案，开发巨灾保险产品，组建巨灾保险共保体，开展巨灾保险试点，人民群众期待已久的巨灾保险制度即将破冰。

服务能力不断提升

保险业以服务经济社会大局作为行业的使命和责任，在完善社会保障体系、参与社会管理、服务"三农"、支持经济发展等方面的作用进一步增强。2014年，保险业为全社会提供风险保障1 114万亿元，同比增长25.5%，赔款与给付7 194.4亿元，同比增长15.9%，服务能力再上新台阶。大病保险在27个省开展392个统筹项目，覆盖人口达7亿人。各类医疗保障经办服务人数达3.2亿人。责任保险保费收入253.4亿元，提供风险保障66.5万亿元。农业保险保费收入325.8亿元，同比增长6.3%，承保金额1.6万亿元，同比增长17.7%。保险资金发起基础设施投资计划1.1万亿元，较年初增长56.8%，其中投资1 072.5亿元参与棚户区改造和保障房建设。出口信用保险保费收入27亿美元，同比增长8.2%，承保总金额达3 804.5亿美元，为稳定国家外需作出了积极贡献。

风险防范不断强化

面对极为复杂的内外部形势，中国保监会科学预判、主动作为，突出"两个加强、两个遏制"，守住了不发生区域性、系统性风险的底线。开展公司治理现场检查、农业保险专项检查、大病保险合规性检查和保险中介市场清理整顿工作。推进"反欺诈、反洗钱、反非法集资"工作，初步建立了保险业反洗钱机制。防范满期给付和退保风险、偿付能力不足风险、流动性风险和资金运用风险。保险公司偿付能力溢额达7 207亿元，仅有一家公司偿付能力不达标。

消费者利益保护工作不断增强

保险业扎实开展保险消费者权益保护工作，着力解决好消费者最关心、最直接、最现实的利益问题。继续治理车险理赔难和寿险销售误导，清理财产保险积压未决赔案735万件。严格落实人身险客户信息真实性管理制度，督促公司加大对销售误导行为的责任追究力度。指导保险行业协会开展人身险公司服务评价和满意度调查，督促公司改进服务质量。妥善解决保险消费争议，12378热线全国转人工呼入总量24.5万个，群众满意度98.5%。保险监管机关全年共

处理各类保险消费投诉2.8万件。推进保险消费者权益保护的制度建设，发布《中国保监会关于加强保险消费者权益保护工作的意见》，制定《中国保险业信用体系建设规划（2015—2020年）》。建设完成官方网站、报纸专栏、普及读物、官方微博、官方微信、现场活动六位一体的保险知识普及渠道。

监管现代化建设稳步推进

一年来，保险监管立足中国国情，把握国际保险监管趋势，积极推进保险监管体系现代化。监管制度建设取得新成绩，基本完成《保险法》修改条文初稿起草工作。推进保险规章废改立，全年修订发布4部行政规章，废止规范性文件1 798件，规范性文件减少近80%。第二代偿付能力监管制度体系基本建成，完成全部主干技术标准共17项监管规则的研制工作，搭建起一套以风险为导向、符合国情、国际可比的新的偿付能力监管体系。监管交流合作不断增强，积极参与国际保险监督官协会共同框架制定和实地测试，保险全球资本标准制定和全球系统重要性保险机构认定相关工作。加强与港澳保险监管机构反保险欺诈监管合作，加上前期签署的《海峡两岸反保险欺诈合作谅解备忘录》，形成了两岸四地共同打击保险欺诈的跨区域长效合作机制。

总的来看，2014年保险业攻坚克难、改革创新，实现了一系列历史性突破。行业整体实力显著增强，社会地位和形象大幅提升，监管的国际话语权不断扩大，保险业已经成为服务国家治理体系和治理能力现代化的重要生力军，中国已经成为影响全球保险格局的重要力量。这些成就的取得，是党中央、国务院正确领导的结果，是相关部委和地方政府大力支持的结果，也凝聚了全系统广大监管干部的辛勤劳动和艰苦努力。在此，我代表中国保监会党委，向辛勤工作的保险从业人员表示亲切的慰问和衷心的感谢，向长期以来关心、支持保险业改革发展的社会各界人士表示诚挚的谢意！

2015年是全面完成"十二五"规划的收官之年，是全面深化改革的关键之年，也是全面推进依法治国和从严治党的开局之年，做好经济工作意义重大。中国保监会将全面贯彻党的十八大和十八届三中、四中全会精神，坚持稳中求进工作总基调，坚持以提高经济发展质量和效益为中心，主动适应经济发展新常态，推动保险业发展保持在合理较快的区间，加强创新驱动，完善风险防控，促进行业发展和保险监管工作更上新台阶，为服务经济社会发展作出新的更大贡献。

中国保险监督管理委员会主席

2015年6月22日

保险系统员工摄影作品

保险系统员工摄影作品

02

经济社会的进步和发展

- 经济运行稳中有进，进一步奠定保险业发展基础
- 社会事业持续推进，有效拓宽保险业发展空间
- 金融市场运行总体平稳，服务经济社会能力进一步增强

2014年，国际、国内环境复杂严峻。全球经济复苏艰难曲折，主要经济体走势分化。国内经济下行压力持续加大，多重困难和挑战相互交织。在以习近平同志为总书记的党中央坚强领导下，全国各族人民万众一心、克难攻坚，完成了全年经济社会发展主要目标任务，全面建成小康社会迈出坚实步伐，全面深化改革实现良好开局，全面依法治国开启新征程，全面从严治党取得新进展。

经济运行稳中有进，进一步奠定保险业发展基础

2014年，中国政府坚持稳中求进的工作总基调，团结带领全国各族人民，科学认识新常态、主动适应新常态、积极引领新常态，改革创新、奋力拼搏，国民经济呈现出增长平稳、结构优化、质量提升、民生改善的良好态势，为保险业发展进一步奠定基础。

经济运行稳中有进

2014年，我国经济发展总体平稳，稳中有进。经济运行处于合理区间，发展的协调性和可持续性增强。国内生产总值达到63.6万亿元，比上年增长7.4%。全年全国一般公共财政收入14万亿元，比上年增长8.6%，其中税收收入11.9万亿元，比上年增长7.8%。国家外汇储备3.8万亿美元，比上年末增加217亿美元。

改革开放持续深化

2014年，通过全面深化改革，市场活力得到释放，有效地对冲了经济下行压力。扎实推动重点领域改革，制订并实施深化财税体制改革总体方案，预算管理制度和税制改革取得重要进展；存款利率和汇率浮动区间扩大，民营银行试点迈出新步伐；能源、交通、环保、通信等领域价格改革加快。继续简政放权，国务院各部门全年取消和下放246项行政审批事项，取消评比达标表彰项目29项、职业资格许可和认定事项149项，再次修订投资项目核准目录，大幅缩减核准范围。着力改革商事制度，新登记注册市场主体达到1 293万户。扩展上海自由贸易试验区范围，新设广东、天津、福建自由贸易试验区。实际使用外商直接投资1 196亿美元，对外直接投资1 029亿美元。中国与冰岛、瑞士自由贸易区启动实施，中韩、中澳自由贸易区完成实质性谈判。铁路、电力、油气、通信等领域对外合作取得重要成果。

结构调整力度进一步加大

2014年，在结构性矛盾突出的情况下，中国政府积极作为，有扶有控，夯实经济社会发展根基。大力调整产业结构，着力培育新的增长点，促进服务业加快发展。支持发展移动互联网、集成电路、高端装备制造、新能源汽车等战略性新兴产业，互联网金融异军突起，电子商务、物流快递等新业态快速成长，文化创意产业蓬勃发展。同时，继续化解过剩产能，推动钢铁、水泥等

15个重点行业淘汰落后产能,年度任务如期完成。加强雾霾治理,淘汰黄标车和老旧车指标超额完成。实施创新驱动发展战略,着力打通科技成果转化通道,扩大中关村国家自主创新示范区试点政策实施范围。超级计算、探月工程、卫星应用等重大科研项目取得新突破,我国自主研制的支线客机飞上蓝天。

农业基础地位不断巩固

2014年,国家加大强农、惠农、富农政策力度,不断巩固农业基础地位。粮食产量实现"十一连增"、农民收入实现"五连快"。全年粮食产量达60 710万吨,比上年增加516万吨,增产0.9%。农业综合生产能力稳步提高,农业科技和机械化水平持续提升,重大水利工程建设进度加快,新增节水灌溉面积223万公顷,新建改建农村公路23万公里。新一轮退耕还林还草启动实施。农村土地确权登记颁证有序进行,农业新型经营主体加快成长。

社会事业持续推进,有效拓宽保险业发展空间

2014年,中国政府始终以增进民生福祉为目的,持续推进民生改善和社会建设,有效拓宽了保险业发展空间。

人民生活水平持续提高

2014年,全国城乡居民收入继续增加。全国居民人均可支配收入实际增长8%。其中,城镇居民人均可支配收入28 844元,实际增长6.8%;农村居民人均可支配收入10 489元,实际增长9.2%。居民消费水平持续提高。全年社会消费品零售总额达到26万亿元,实际增长10.9%,其中,城镇消费品零售额增长11.8%;乡村消费品零售额增长12.9%。限额以上企业商品零售额中,通信器材类零售额增长达到32.7%,金银珠宝类与上年持平,家具类、化妆品类等热点消费领域零售额均实现了10%以上的增长,汽车类零售额也增长了7.7%,年末全国民用轿车保有量8 307万辆,增长16.6%。农村贫困人口减少1 232万人,6 600多万农村人口饮水安全问题得到解决,出境旅游超过1亿人次。

保障和改善民生力度加大

2014年,全国就业持续增加,全年城镇新增就业1 322万人,年末城镇登记失业率为4.09%。全年全国城镇保障性安居工程基本建成住房511万套,新开工740万套。教育科技和文化体育事业较快发展。全年研究生招生62.1万人,普通本专科招生721.4万人,全年研究与试验发展经费支出13 312亿元,比上年增长12.4%。国家坚持以人为本,持续增加民生投入,保基本、兜底线、建机制,财政用于民生的比例达到70%以上。

社会保障体系建设取得新进展

2014年，社会保障体系建设取得新进展。全国参加城镇职工基本养老保险人数比上年末增加1 897万人，参加城乡居民基本养老保险人数增加357万人。参加基本医疗保险、失业保险、工伤保险、生育保险的人数比上年分别增加2 702万人、626万人、703万人、643万人。启动实施新型农村合作医疗和城镇居民基本医疗保险"并轨"，企业退休人员基本养老金水平提高10%。全年资助1 310.9万城市困难群众参加医疗保险，资助4 118.9万农村困难群众参加新型农村合作医疗。全面建立临时救助制度，城乡低保标准分别提高9.97%和14.1%。

金融市场运行总体平稳，服务经济社会能力进一步增强

2014年，金融市场运行总体平稳，各项改革和发展措施稳步推进，金融市场对于降低社会融资成本、促进实体经济发展的作用得以进一步发挥。

继续实施稳健货币政策，全面深化金融改革开放

2014年，国家继续实施稳健的货币政策，不断补充和完善货币政策工具组合，保持货币供应总量松紧适度，引导金融机构盘活存量、用好增量，建立和引导金融机构加大对"三农"、小微企业、棚户区改造、铁路等重点行业和领域的支持，拓宽企业直接融资渠道。2014年M2增长12.2%，人民币贷款新增9.78万亿元，同比增加8 900亿元，全年的社会融资规模接近16.5万亿元。在金融改革方面，积极稳妥地推进金融重点领域和关键环节的改革，充分发挥市场在资源配置中的决定性作用，利率和汇率的市场化改革进一步推进，人民币跨境使用明显加快，资本项目可兑换迈出新步伐，存款保险制度建设取得实质性进展。

银行业经营发展保持稳健态势

2014年，我国银行业各项经营管理和风险监管指标稳步向好，资产和负债规模稳步增长，资本充足率继续维持在较高水平。截至2014年末，银行业金融机构资产总额为172.3万亿元，同比增长13.87%。商业银行全年累计实现净利润1.55万亿元，同比增长9.65%；平均资产利润率为1.23%。商业银行加权平均资本充足率为13.18%，较年初上升0.99个百分点。不良贷款余额为8 426亿元，较上年末增加2 506亿元；商业银行不良贷款率为1.25%，较上年末上升0.25个百分点。

资本市场运行总体平稳，多层次资本市场建设取得重要突破

2014年，中国资本市场运行总体平稳。基础制度市场化改革不断深化，并购重组和退市等制度日益完善。沪港通试点正式启动，新三板挂牌企业数量顺利突破1 500家，多层次资本

市场正在加速形成。全年上市公司通过境内市场累计筹资8 397亿元，比上年增加1 512亿元。2014年末，上证综合指数和深证综合指数分别收于3 234点和1 415点，比上年末分别上升52.8%和33.7%，创业板指数收于1 471点，比上年末上升12.8%。

保险市场实现强势发展，服务大局能力不断提升

2014年，保险市场实现强势发展，行业发展活力极大激发，服务大局能力不断提升，行业驶入发展快车道。保险费率形成机制改革稳步推进，万能保险费率市场化改革和商业车险条款费率管理制度改革即将落地。市场准入退出制度改革进一步完善，保险资金配置多元化格局基本形成，巨灾保险制度建设取得积极进展，偿二代监管制度体系基本建成，保险消费者权益保护工作取得新进展。2014年保险公司偿付能力溢额为7 207亿元，仅有一家保险公司偿付能力不达标。全国保费收入突破2万亿元，同比增长17.5%。保险业总资产突破10万亿元，较年初增长22.3%。

保险系统员工摄影作品

保险系统员工摄影作品

03

保险业服务经济社会发展

· 推动提高医疗保障水平

· 参与完善多层次养老保障体系

· 创新社会管理机制

· 参与完善灾害事故防范救助体系

· 积极服务"三农"

· 促进经济提质增效升级

· 积极履行社会责任

推动提高医疗保障水平

开展城乡居民大病保险 2014年，中国保监会积极推进城乡居民大病保险工作，着力完善全民医保体系建设。截至2014年末，除西藏外，各地大病保险工作陆续启动。16家保险公司在全国27个省（区、市）265个地市（含新疆兵团14个师）的2 128个县区（含新疆兵团175个团场）开展大病保险，覆盖人口7亿人，占应覆盖人数的近70%。大病保险保费收入154.4亿元，赔付197万人次。目前，大病保险最高补偿超过80万元，次均赔付约为5 600元。患者实际报销费用比例在原基本医保基础上普遍增加了10-15个百分点，达到70%左右，支付赔款111亿元，有力地缓解了"因病致贫、因病返贫"现象。

发展商业健康保险 针对群众基本医疗保障之上更高层次的健康保障需求，保险机构通过扩大商业健康保险产品供给，使广大人民群众拥有健全的健康风险保障。2014年，100多家保险公司开展商业健康保险业务，健康保险产品覆盖疾病险、医疗险、护理险和失能收入损失险四大类，在售产品2 300多个，保费收入1 586.3亿元，同比增长41.9%，赔付支出572.4亿元。保险业在大力发展健康险业务的同时，积极探索与健康管理相结合，从简单的费用报销和经济补偿，向病前、病中、病后的综合性健康保障管理方向发展，提高了参保群众健康水平。

参与基本医疗保障管理 保险业借助自身在精算技术、专业服务和风险管理等方面的优势，主动承担社会责任，接受政府委托，积极稳妥地参与新农合、城镇居民基本医疗等各类基本医疗保障经办管理，降低了经办管理成本，管控了医疗费用，减少了财政支出，提高了基本医保经办服务质量和效率，较好地发挥了社会管理作用。2014年末，保险业参与各类医保经办服务人数达3.2亿人次，新增受托管理基金189.2亿元，为3 611.6万人次支付赔款135.2亿元；提供城镇职工补充医疗、企事业团体补充医疗、医疗救助等健康保险专项服务，保费收入145.3亿元，赔付支出144.5亿元。

专栏一　国务院办公厅印发《关于加快发展商业健康保险的若干意见》

2014年11月17日，国务院办公厅发布了《关于加快发展商业健康保险的若干意见》，这是我国经济社会进入新常态后，国家从战略高度创新改革思路，运用市场机制深入推进医疗改革、积极破解经济社会发展难题、保障和改善民生的有力举措。

《意见》明确了今后较长一段时期商业健康保险发展的指导思想、目标和基本原则，提出了完善发展商业健康保险的支持政策，同时，就加强组织领导和部门协同，营造良好社会氛围等提出了要求。《意见》必将对完善我国医疗保障体系、促进深化医改、推进健康产业发展带来深远影响。

广东省实现大病保险全覆盖

截至2014年末，广东省大病保险实现全省覆盖，全部地市达到市级统筹，城乡一体。其中商业保险公司承办了18个地市的大病保险业务，覆盖超过110个县区，保障人数超过6 000万人。政府与市场的有机衔接，使住院政策范围内报销比例较制度实施前提高14.3个百分点，实际赔付比例超过50%。

阳光保险获准筹建国内首家险企投资医院

2014年5月，阳光保险集团获准投资筹建阳光融和医院，这是国内首家由保险机构和国有大型医院及教学机构合作兴办的股份制医院。项目总投入25亿元，占地900亩，已建成一期医院门诊、住院综合楼28万平方米，床位2 000张。

参与完善多层次养老保障体系

2014年，中国保监会认真贯彻落实国务院部署和要求，推动保险业发挥专业化和市场化管理优势，服务多层次养老保障体系建设，取得了积极成效。

试点参与基本养老保险经办管理 保险公司发挥自身专业优势，积极参与试点，提供经办服务。截至2014年末，保险业承接了江苏宜兴市、四川德阳市旌阳区、浙江衢州市衢江区、江苏楚州和连云港、四川什坊和绵竹等地的新农保经办服务工作，共计服务132万人。

保险业参与基本养老保险经办管理，开创了"政府主导、管办分离、市场运作、专业服务"的新型运营模式。一是改进公共服务的提供方式。二是减轻政府增设经办机构及人员编制压力，降低行政成本。三是通过保险公司的技术、人才和网络，实现了全程信息化管理和严格的风险控制，提高了服务水平和工作效率。

2014年6月25日，海康人寿联合清华大学发布"2014年中国居民退休准备指数"。

专栏二 老年人住房反向抵押养老保险试点启动

2014年6月，中国保监会发布《关于开展老年人住房反向抵押养老保险试点的指导意见》，决定从2014年7月1日起在北京、上海、广州、武汉四地开展老年人住房反向抵押养老保险试点。

老年人住房反向抵押养老保险是一种将住房抵押与终身年金相结合的创新型商业养老保险业务。拥有房屋完全产权的老年人，将其房屋抵押给保险公司，继续拥有房屋占有、使用、收益和经抵押权人同意的处置权，并按照约定条件领取养老金直至身故；老人身故后，保险公司获得抵押房屋处置权，处置所得将优先用于偿付养老保险相关费用。发展住房反向抵押养老保险，将社会存量资产转化为养老资源，丰富了养老保障方式，开拓了保险业参与养老服务业发展的空间。

苏州建立新型养老服务风险分担机制

2014年，苏州建立新型养老服务风险分担机制，由政府出资购买三项惠老保险，包括养老机构综合责任保险、居家养老服务组织责任保险和老年人意外伤害保险，构建了保险参与养老体系建设的新机制。全年保险机构共为全市62.5万名老人提供106亿元意外风险保障，为全市95个街道4.1万张次养老床位提供34亿元风险保障。

为企业年金提供全程管理服务　保险业发挥在方案咨询与设计、客户服务、稳健投资等方面的优势，为企业年金计划的发起、运营、给付提供全程服务，承担了受托管理人、账户管理人和投资管理人等多种角色。截至2014年末，保险业在企业年金市场共计为4.3万家企业提供受托管理服务，覆盖877万人，累计受托管理资产3 174.2亿元，受托资产规模占法人受托业务的68.8%；管理企业账户9 845个，个人账户252万个；投资管理资产余额3 753.7亿元，占企业年金基金实际投资运作金额的50.7%。

积极推动商业年金保险发展　商业保险通过向社会提供多样化的养老年金保险产品和服务，有效地弥补了社会养老保障的不足。目前，我国商业年金保险业务经营主体有69家，年金保险产品种类丰富。近年来，年金保险一直保持较快发展速度，2001-2014年保费收入年均增长16.9%。2014年，年金保险保费收入2 822亿元，同比增长77.2%，有效保单6 943.3万件，覆盖1亿人次，保额达到1.4万亿元。

创新社会管理机制

2014年，保险业通过大力发展责任保险，参与创新社会管理机制，有效分散社会风险、化解社会矛盾、减轻政府压力、维护社会稳定。全年责任保险实现保费收入253.4亿元，提供风险保障金额66.5万亿元。

大力发展医疗责任保险，创新医患纠纷调处机制

保险业积极发展医疗责任保险，通过建立以人民调解为主体，院内调解、司法调解、医疗风险分担机制有机结合、相互衔接的"三调解一保险"的医疗纠纷预防与处理制度，缓解医患矛盾，维护正常的医疗秩序。2014年中国保监会联合卫计委、财政部等5部委印发《关于加强医疗责任保险工作的意见》，并会同卫计委等部门开展创建"平安医院"全国督查工作。

> **天津大力推动医疗责任险发展**
>
> 2014年，天津保监局积极推动医疗责任保险发展，服务国家治理体系和治理能力现代化。推动出台《天津市医疗纠纷处置条例》（以下简称《条例》），根据《条例》的规定，天津市二级以上公立医疗机构须参保医疗责任险。截至2014年末，天津保险机构累计为全市81家医疗机构提供风险保障5.9亿元，处理赔案3 868件，赔付支出2.1亿元，医疗纠纷调解成功率达87.5%。

大力发展产品质量安全责任保险，加强产品质量安全管理

为建立完善符合市场规律的产品质量安全多元救济和产品侵权责任制度，保险业大力发展产品质量安全责任保险。2014年，中国保监会联合国家质检总局印发《关于开展产品质量安全责任保险工作的通知》，鼓励支持在特种设备、重点消费领域探索实施产品质量安全责任保险制度。大力发展产品质量安全责任保险，对于保障人民群众合法权益、维护社会和谐安定、提高企业风险管理能力具有重要意义。

大力发展食品安全责任保险，保障食品药品安全

2014年，中国保监会与国务院食品安全办、食药总局联合发布《关于开展食品安全责任保险试点工作的指导意见》，将食品安全责任保险试点情况纳入地方食品安全工作考核评价体系，企业投保情况纳入企业信用记录和分级分类管理指标体系。

> **湖南开展食品安全责任强制保险试点**
>
> 2014年，湖南省在生产企业、食堂和餐饮服务等领域启动食品安全责任强制保险试点工作，全年累计签单1 371笔，为897个食堂、417家生产企业、57家餐饮企业提供了14.8亿元风险保障。

大力发展环境污染责任保险，完善生态环境保护管理体制

2014年，环境污染责任保险制度建设迈出重大步伐，新修订的《环境保护法》将鼓励投保环境污染责任保险作为重要内容。中国保监会与环保部联合印发《关于开展环境污染强制责任保险试点工作的指导意见》，在涉重金属企业和石油化工等高环境风险行业启动强制保险试点。推动制定化工、金属冶炼等6个行业环境污染责任保险风险评估标准，逐步健全环境污染责任保险技术规范体系。指导行业协会推出环境污染责任保险示范条款，为企业提供全面风险保障。

参与完善灾害事故防范救助体系

完成制度顶层设计，为巨灾保险提供法律保障

2014年，中国保监会联合财政部制定《完善保险经济补偿机制 建立巨灾保险制度工作方案》，并成立巨灾保险制度课题研究组，形成了《建立巨灾保险制度课题研究报告》及其子报告《建立我国地震巨灾保险制度试运行方案》，完成了巨灾保险制度的顶层设计。

在充分考虑我国实际情况和巨灾保险现实需求的基础上，中国保监会选取地震保险作为巨灾保险的立法突破点，制定《地震巨灾保险条例》。《地震巨灾保险条例》从法律层面明确政府与市场合作的巨灾保险运行模式、参与地震巨灾保险制度各主体间的权利义务、地震巨灾保险制度的组织形式、核心机构的组建方式及巨灾保险经营规则和经营风险防范，为巨灾保险制度的顺利实施提供法律保障。

探索地震巨灾保险制度试行方案，推动地震保险落地实施

2014年，保险业通过开发示范产品、搭建制度、完善风险分散机制，积极推动地震保险落地。开发全国住宅地震保险示范产品，该产品以城乡居民住房为保障对象，按城乡确定不同保险金额，实现"广覆盖、保基本"。组建地震保险共保体，制订共保体筹备工作方案、拟定共保体章程，推进共保体成立相关事宜。研究建立地震巨灾保险基金，按照地震巨灾保险保费收入或超额承保利润的一定比例计提地震巨灾保险基金。在专门管理机构成立前选择代管机构，对地震巨灾保险基金实行专户管理、独立核算、逐年滚存、全国统筹。

开展巨灾保险试点，为巨灾保险推广积累经验

继深圳开展巨灾保险试点之后，2014年，巨灾保险试点进一步扩容，宁波巨灾保险正式实施。宁波巨灾保险体系由公共巨灾保险、巨灾基金和商业巨灾保险三部分组成，其中公共巨灾保险中首次涉及了家庭财产损失救助领域。与此同时，云南、上海、广东等地也在研究制订符合当地特点的巨灾保险制度试点方案。

中华财险在成都开展农房险试点

2014年，中华财险在成都11个区县试点农房保险，保险责任范围涵盖地震巨灾风险及暴雨、洪水、火灾等15种一般风险。截至2014年底，成都农房险承保覆盖面近30%，为成都近45万户农户提供272亿元的巨灾保障。

诚泰财险联手云南财经大学
建立巨灾风险管理研究中心

2014年12月，诚泰财险与云南财经大学合作共建的巨灾风险管理研究中心揭牌成立。该中心为开放式保险技术研发运用平台，主要致力于巨灾风险管理智库服务、巨灾风险管理保险技术研发创新、支持企业巨灾风险管理业务发展以及保险风险管理人才培养。

积极服务"三农"

2014年，农业保险在国家支农、惠农政策的支持下，继续保持平稳较快发展态势，在保障农业生产稳定、提高农民抗灾救灾能力、稳定农民收入、保障国家粮食安全等方面发挥了重要作用。

服务领域不断拓展　2014年，我国农业保险累计实现保费收入325.8亿元，同比增长6.3%；参保农户2.5亿户次，同比增长15.7%；提供风险保障1.6万亿元，同比增长17.7%；农业保险赔款214.6亿元，同比增长2.9%；受益农户3 244.6万户次，同比增长2.1%。农业保险承保主要农作物11.7亿亩，占全国主要农作物播种面积的47.7%，其中，玉米、水稻、小麦三大口粮作物覆盖率分别达68.7%、69.5%和49.3%，承保森林21.7亿亩，覆盖率达67.2%；承保育肥猪1.3亿头，奶牛398.1万头，同比分别增长54.3%和21.2%。

市场秩序日益规范　2014年，中国保监会联合财政部全面开展农业保险检查工作，共对全国11家产险法人机构开展检查。通过检查有效遏制了虚假承保、虚假理赔等侵害国家和农民利益的违法、违规行为，确保国家补贴资金真正用之于民。

制度与基础建设不断加强　2014年，中国保监会不断加强农业保险制度与基础建设工作力度。取消农业保险业务经营资格审批，构建适度竞争的市场格局；完善农业保险管理制度，加强产品监管，与财政部、农业部联合拟订《关于进一步完善中央财政保费补贴型农业保险产品条款拟定工作的通知》，强化条款设计和费率厘定的合法性和公平性审查，建立费率和保额动态调整机制；加强农业保险基础建设，启动全国农业保险管理信息平台建设，推动建立中国农业保险再保险共同体。

专栏三　中国农业保险再保险共同体成立

2014年11月21日，中国农业保险再保险共同体成立。中国农业保险再保险共同体由境内23家具有农业保险经营资质的保险公司和中国财产再保险公司共同发起组建，业务保障范围包括现有的所有农业保险业务。中国农业保险再保险共同体的成立，进一步完善了我国农业大灾风险转移分散机制，确保我国农业保险再保险分散渠道的稳定。

政策环境日趋优化　2014年，中央财政本级农业保险保费补贴预算同比增长20%。中国保监会会同财政部、国家税务总局将农业保险所得税优惠政策延续至2016年底。育肥猪保险补贴比例从10%提高到50%，奶牛保险补贴区域新增4省，育肥猪保险补贴区域新增2省，森林保险补贴区域新增2省。积极开展目标价格保险试点，2014年已拓展到20个省市。

国内首份《农险需求调查报告》发布

2014年9月10日,中国保险学会发布《农险需求调查报告》。报告通过对一万多个调查样本的统计分析,深入研究了我国农户、农业经济组织、基层政府的风险状况,农业保险覆盖情况,对农业保险的认识与接受水平以及对农业保险与服务的需求。报告为进一步完善我国农业保险支持政策、提升农业保险覆盖与保障水平、优化农业保险服务体系和服务能力提出了有针对性的建议。

安信农险推出蔬菜气象指数保险

2014年,安信农险积极探索气象指数保险在农业领域的应用,推出蔬菜气象指数保险,将一个或几个气候条件对农作物损害程度指数化,保险合同以这种指数为基础,达到约定理赔条件时,投保人就可以获得相应赔偿。该保险产品管理成本低,保险公司并不需要复杂的理赔技术和程序,保户可直接按照公布的指数领取赔偿金,解决了信息不对称、逆选择和道德风险问题。该险种已为32家农业合作社提供保险保障655万元,及时为受损菜农提供补偿,保障了菜农的生产积极性。

促进经济提质增效升级

提质增效是新常态下经济发展的关键之举。2014年,保险业认真贯彻落实党中央、国务院部署,不断加大支持实体经济发展的力度,促进经济转型升级,取得了显著成效。

全力支持经济建设,满足实体经济融资需求

截至2014年末,保险资金已经为交通、能源、铁路、重大水利工程等基础设施建设以及棚户区改造、保障房、养老社区等民生工程提供超过万亿元资金支持。累计发起设立各类债权、股权和项目资产支持计划378项,合计备案(注册)金额10 644.4亿元。

在投资方式和产品形式多样化方面,保险资金除投资基础设施债权投资

中国人保发起设立全国首个
金融央企与省级政府合作股权基金

中国人保发起设立全国首个金融央企与省级政府合作股权基金——规模为121亿元的广东(人保)粤东西北振兴发展股权基金,重点投资粤东西北地级市(含肇庆)的新区及中心城区的扩容提质项目,支持广东省区域协调发展。

计划外,正在加快发展股权投资计划、项目资产支持计划和股权投资基金等方式。在交易结构上,已经逐步从债权、股权等较为单一的交易结构,逐步向股债结合、优先股等更为灵活的交易结构发展,满足实体经济多样化的融资需求。

专栏四　中国保监会印发《保险业服务新型城镇化发展的指导意见》

　　2014年3月，为深入贯彻落实中央城镇化工作会议精神和《中共中央国务院关于印发〈国家新型城镇化规划（2014—2020年）〉的通知》要求，中国保监会出台了《保险业服务新型城镇化发展的指导意见》。《保险业服务新型城镇化发展的指导意见》从统筹发展商业养老保险和医疗健康保险、完善多层次社会保障体系，创新保险资金运用形式、支持新型城镇化建设，发挥保险机制作用、促进城市经济持续健康发展，加强社会风险管理、创新城市社会治理，健全农业保险服务体系、促进新型城镇化与农业现代化协调发展，深化改革创新、提升保险服务质量和水平六个方面对保险业提出了意见要求。

大力发展信用保证保险，助力小微企业融资发展

　　为进一步发挥保险功能作用，支持小微企业发展，2014年，中国保监会会同工业和信息化部、商务部、中国人民银行和中国银监会研究起草关于发展信用保证保险，服务支持小微企业方面的指导意见，以充分发挥信用保证保险的融资增信功能，缓解小微企业融资难、融资贵问题。指导意见鼓励银行对购买信用保险和贷款保证保险进行贷款的小微企业给予贷款优惠政策，试点放开经营小微企业业务达到一定规模的保险公司接入人民银行征信系统，实现信息共享。

　　2014年，保险业以宁波小额贷款保证保险试点为典型，以"政府主导，市场化运作、风险共担"为基础，创新 "政府+银行+保险"的合作模式，全面推广小额贷款保证保险试点工作。自2009年至2014年底，全国已有21个省（自治区、直辖市）、48个地级市（区）相继开展小额贷款保证保险试点工作，其中，浙江、广西、云南等9省（区）以省（区）政府名义陆续出台小额贷款保证保险试点工作的指导性文件。2014年，小额贷款保证保险累计支持8.4万家小微企业获得融资贷款229亿元。

　　2014年9月18日，中国保监会、宁波市政府联合召开"保险业支持小微企业发展暨'宁波经验'交流会"，共同探讨保险业支持小微企业的发展思路。中国保监会项俊波主席、陈文辉副主席及宁波市领导出席会议，工业和信息化部、中国银监会等4部委和12个省市金融办受邀参会。

推动短期出口信用保险发展，帮助企业"走出去"

　　大力推动短期出口信用保险，为企业提供出口收汇风险保障，能够提升我国出口企业的国际竞争力。在借鉴国外成熟经验的基础上，自2013年开始，中国保监会会同财政部、商务部等

部门，逐步引入4家商业保险机构，试点经营短期出口信用保险业务，推动市场化进程。2014年，我国短期出口信用保险实现保费收入11.8亿美元，承保金额3 602亿美元，累计服务支持出口企业超过5.3万家，获得融资额度2 125.8亿元，其中为3.7万家出口小微企业获得融资额度252.3亿元。

积极履行社会责任

2014年，保险业积极履行社会责任，秉承大爱无疆的理念，开展一系列教育、医疗、灾难救助等公益事业，充分彰显保险业"人人为我，我为人人"的精神。

专栏五　首份《中国保险业社会责任白皮书》发布

2014年7月8日，中国保监会向社会发布首份《中国保险业社会责任白皮书》。白皮书系统梳理了保险业在服务国家经济转型、助力社会保障体系建设、构建灾害救助体系和参与社会管理创新等方面所发挥的作用，展示了保险业近年来在农业保险、巨灾保险、责任保险和大病保险等方面的发展情况和主要成绩，充分展现了行业积极践行社会责任所做的工作。

中国人寿履行社会责任　积极参与慈善救助

2014年，中国人寿慈善基金会全年对外捐赠3 600多万元，主要用于助养汶川地震、玉树地震和舟曲泥石流致孤儿童；支持湖北郧西县和广西天等县、龙州县的扶贫项目；救助失独家庭；在辽宁省部分农村地区援建基层卫生院肾病透析室；为宁夏南部山区部分乡镇医院配备急救车和彩色B超医疗设备；支持为贫困地区女性提供"两癌筛查"及重大疾病保障等。

泰康养老联合挂号网推行"医者无忧"计划

2014年10月18日，泰康养老携手挂号网推出"医者无忧"保障计划，为执业医师提供5万元的意外伤害保险和5 000元的意外医疗保险，目前已有逾万名医生参与到计划中。该计划与互联网技术深度融合，执业医师只需在挂号网注册，就可通过该网站或微医移动客户端免费申领。

华夏保险启动"致敬抗战老兵"公益项目

2014年，华夏保险依托与中国青少年发展基金会、中国老龄事业发展基金会共同成立的"华夏慈善基金"，捐赠260余万元启动"致敬抗战老兵"公益项目，在全国寻访抗战老兵，为他们发放生活补助、颁发抗战荣誉证书和勋章，并拍摄口述历史。

安邦养老保险"重阳"敬老院送祝福

2014年重阳节期间，安邦养老保险员工组成爱心联盟志愿者团队，走访京、津地区近十家敬老院，为近千名老人送去笔记本电脑、血压计、血糖仪、食用油等医疗和日常生活用品。

利宝保险关注儿童安全　普及道路安全知识

2014年，为普及儿童安全知识，利宝保险先后在金华、北京、济南、广州4地举办了"安全出行好成长"儿童道路安全活动。利宝保险儿童安全项目自2012年启动以来，已在多个城市成功推进。

保险系统员工摄影作品

保险系统员工摄影作品

04

保险监管

基本情况

中国保险监督管理委员会主要职责

1. 拟定保险业发展的方针政策，制订行业发展战略和规划；起草保险业监管的法律、法规；制定业内规章。

2. 审批保险公司及其分支机构、保险集团公司、保险控股公司的设立；会同有关部门审批保险资产管理公司的设立；审批境外保险机构代表处的设立；审批保险代理公司、保险经纪公司、保险公估公司等保险中介机构及其分支机构的设立；审批境内保险机构和非保险机构在境外设立保险机构；审批保险机构的合并、分立、变更、解散，决定接管和指定接受；参与、组织保险公司的破产、清算。

3. 审查、认定各类保险机构高级管理人员的任职资格；制定保险从业人员的基本资格标准。

4. 审批关系社会公众利益的保险险种、依法实行强制保险的险种和新开发的人寿保险险种等的保险条款和保险费率，对其他保险险种的保险条款和保险费率实施备案管理。

5. 依法监管保险公司的偿付能力和市场行为；负责保险保障基金的管理，监管保险保证金；根据法律和国家对保险资金的运用政策，制定有关规章制度，依法对保险公司的资金运用进行监管。

6. 对政策性保险和强制保险进行业务监管；对专属自保、相互保险等组织形式和业务活动进行监管。归口管理保险行业协会、保险学会等行业社团组织。

7. 依法对保险机构和保险从业人员的不正当竞争等违法、违规行为以及对非保险机构经营或变相经营保险业务进行调查、处罚。

8. 依法对境内保险及非保险机构在境外设立的保险机构进行监管。

9. 制定保险行业信息化标准；建立保险风险评价、预警和监控体系，跟踪分析、监测、预测保险市场运行状况，负责统一编制全国保险业的数据、报表，并按照国家有关规定予以发布。

10. 承办国务院交办的其他事项。

监管机构的组织框架

	办公厅
	发展改革部
	政策研究室
	财务会计部
副主席	保险消费者权益保护局
纪委书记	财产保险监管部
	人身保险监管部
副主席	保险中介监管部
主席	保险资金运用监管部
副主席	国际部
	法规部
副主席	统计信息部
	稽查局
主席助理	人事教育部
	监察局
	机关党委

　　直属中国保监会的36个派出机构，以及河北唐山、江苏苏州、浙江温州、山东烟台和广东汕头5个保险监管分局，根据授权履行行政管理职能，依照国家有关法律、法规和方针、政策，统一监督管理辖区内的保险市场，维护当地保险市场平稳运行，促进保险业持续健康发展。

监管目标

◎ 保护保单持有人利益
◎ 防范和化解风险
◎ 促进保险业持续健康发展

公司治理监管

2014年，中国保监会继续推进公司治理改革，不断加强和改善公司治理监管，在完善制度建设，改进监管方式及加强集团公司监管等领域都取得了积极成效。

不断加强公司治理制度体系建设

制定《保险法人机构公司治理评价办法》，对保险公司治理水平进行评级分类，将评价结果直接与公司薪酬管理、分支机构准入和业务稽查挂钩，增强评价指标的约束力，并对整改不力的保险法人机构实施黄、红牌警告制度。制定《关于进一步规范保险公司关联交易有关问题的通知》，通过强化关联交易的比例监管、内部审核和信息披露，进一步防范保险公司实际控制人利用关联交易侵占公司中小股东和广大被保险人利益的行为。建立保险公司治理问题数据库，将数据库资料作为治理评价和选择现场检查对象的重要依据。

不断改进公司治理现场和非现场监管

在现场监管方面，继续开展公司治理专项检查工作，在检查对象、检查内容、检查频率等方面进一步扩大规模和范围。根据检查结果，及时向相关公司下发监管函，督促完成整改工作。在非现场监管方面，一是继续开展公司治理年度报告专项分析，对问题公司下发风险提示函，督促及时整改。二是开展公司章程专项检查，对88家有代表性的保险公司现行章程进行了审查梳理，加大对重点公司的专项督导力度，督促相关公司限期整改。

全面监控和防范集团化经营风险

制定《保险公司所属非保险子公司管理暂行办法》，对保险公司所属非保险子公司的风险进行全面监测，防止风险跨公司、跨行业传递。推动开展国内系统重要性保险机构（D-SII）监管，逐步建立与国际监管衔接、具有中国特色的D-SII监管体系。加强对保险集团风险的全面监测，制定发布《保险集团并表监管指引》，明确保险集团并表管理的主体责任。夯实集团监管基础设施，完善保险集团信息报送机制，健全集团监管信息档案，筑牢保险集团非现场监管基础。

专栏六　中国保监会印发《保险公司所属非保险子公司管理暂行办法》

2014年9月，为加强对保险公司所属非保险子公司的监督管理，不断健全对非保险子公司的风险监测机制，中国保监会出台了《保险公司所属非保险子公司管理暂行办法》。《办法》重点规范保险公司投资和管理非保险子公司的五类行为：一是投资设立非保险子公司，二是对非保险子公司的管控，三是与非保险子公司之间的内部交易，四是向非保险子公司的外包，五是与非保险子公司的防火墙建设。《办法》在保险公司进入非保险业务领域的准入条件，保险公司退出非保险业务领域的情形与报告机制方面做了具体规定。

专栏七　《保险集团并表监管指引》出台

2014年12月，为进一步加强保险集团监管，完善对保险集团的并表监管，有效防范保险集团经营风险，中国保监会出台了《保险集团并表监管指引》。《指引》立足于有效防范保险集团风险，在支持保险公司集团化经营，发挥协同作用、规模效应的同时，通过明晰集团结构、监测内部交易，健全全面风险管理体系、风险隔离机制，完善公司治理、信息披露机制，实现对保险集团风险的全面监测。

专栏八　中国保监会加强全球系统重要性保险机构监管

2014年，平安保险集团再次入选全球系统重要性保险机构（G-SII）名单。中国保监会积极参与G-SII认定工作，在深入研究G-SII国际监管制度的基础上，牵头成立了平安集团危机管理小组，指导平安集团建立了系统性风险管理计划和恢复与处置计划。同时，推动开展国内系统重要性保险机构（D-SII）监管工作，研究起草监管框架和相关配套监管文件，逐步建立与国际监管衔接、具有中国特色的D-SII监管体系，提升了我国集团监管的国际话语权。

偿付能力监管

行业偿付能力充足

截至2014年末，行业偿付能力充足，仅有一家保险公司偿付能力不达标，所有达标公司偿付能力均处于充足II类，行业偿付能力状况良好，为进入偿二代过渡期奠定了坚实基础。其中，产险公司偿付能力充足率的中位数为360%，环比上升7个百分点；寿险公司偿付能力充足率的中位数为285%，环比上升21个百分点。

偿付能力溢额大幅提高

2014年末，全行业偿付能力溢额为7 207亿元，环比大幅增加1 656亿元，增幅达30%。行业偿付能力溢额上升主要源于保险资金投资收益表现良好。2014年，保险资金运用实现收益5 358.8亿元，同比增长46.5%，达到5年来最好水平。同时，第四季度共有17家公司增资，总额为304.5亿元。

偿付能力日常监管进一步加强

2014年，中国保监会进一步加强偿付能力日常监管，制定出台了关于高现金价值产品最低资本、历史存量高利率保单资金投资的蓝筹股、证券投资基金和资产管理产品等方面的偿付能力报告编报规则，有效地防范了高现价产品风险、高利率保单利差损风险及保险资金运用风险。发文暂停投资性房地产评估增值政策，开展投资性房地产清理审核工作，防范投资性房地产风险。不断提升偿付能力季度分析预测、预警能力，修改完善偿付能力监管委员会工作程序，提高监管效率。

行业资本补充机制进一步完善

2014年，中国保监会研究起草《保险公司资本补充管理办法（征求意见稿）》，建立由"资本分级、资本工具、公司资本管理、监督检查"组成的行业资本补充机制，规定了普通股、优先股、资本公积等八大类资本补充渠道。建立保险公司资本分级制度，将保险公司资本分为核心一级资本、核心二级资本、附属一级资本和附属二级资本四类，明确各级资本的属性、标准和额度。创新保险公司资本补充工具，积极与有关部委沟通，协商保险公司拓宽融资渠道的可能性和操作性，起草《中国保监会关于保险公司发行优先股有关事项的通知》、《中国人民银行　中国保监会关于保险公司发行资本补充债券有关事项的公告》。

市场行为监管

2014年，面对极为复杂的内外部形势，中国保监会坚持严监管防风险，强化市场行为监管力度，创新现场检查方式，大力整顿和规范市场秩序，守住了不发生区域性、系统性风险底线。

全面强化现场检查

2014年，中国保监会共派出2 586个检查组，对2 739家保险机构、中介机构开展了现场检查。根据检查发现问题，对455家保险机构、中介机构和529名保险从业人员进行了行政处罚，撤销任职资格或从业资格24人，吊销经营许可证13家，责令停止接受新业务11家。此外，根据检查发现问题，对776家保险机构和350名保险从业人员采取了监管谈话、通报批评和下发监管函等其他监管措施。

重点实施三大领域专项检查

一是中国保监会联合财政部开展农业保险专项检查，覆盖11家产险机构的166家分支机构，严查虚假承保、虚假理赔等侵害国家和农民利益的违法违规行为。二是在全国范围开展大病保险合规性检查，成立3个总公司检查组和30个省级检查组，首次大规模采取异地交叉检查方式，重点检查121个大病保险项目，全面摸清大病保险试点以来经营情况，确保该项惠民政策的规范运行。三是全面开展保险中介市场清理整顿工作，对135家保险公司、1 745家保险省级分公司、2 530家保险专业中介机构、617家金融类兼业代理机构进行了清查。专项大检查的实施，震慑了不法行为，树立了监管权威，是保险监管方式的重要创新。

> **山西保监局加强县域市场监管巡查**
>
> 山西保监局围绕监管工作重点，按季度深入县域市场开展监管巡查，全年实现对全省119个县市区的全覆盖。通过巡查，摸清了基层保险市场情况，推动农业保险、大病保险等惠民保险更好地服务地方经济。

全流程防范化解案件风险

2014年，中国保监会采取有力措施，初步化解了大案要案风险。事前强化防控。坚持打早打小，对65家人身保险公司开展资金案件风险排查。通报典型案件，交流经验，促进行业提升案件风险防控能力。事中稳妥处置。先后边控17人次，有效防控案件责任人转移资金、潜逃海外等风险。事后严肃警示。指导协调保险机构完成151起案件共403人的责任追究，倒逼保险机构高管增强责任意识和风险防范意识；完成30多起大案要案调查，责成10家保险公司针对案件暴露的问题排查风险，有效堵塞制度管控漏洞。

稳步推进"反欺诈、反洗钱、处置非法集资"工作

中国保监会联合公安部门在浙江、福建、宁波、厦门两省四地启动了打击保险欺诈犯罪的"安宁行动"，向公安部门移送保险欺诈线索共计5 599条，协助公安机关侦破保险诈骗犯罪案件184起，打击犯罪团伙29个，涉案金额近1 900万元。在西安成功举办第三届海峡两岸反保险欺诈研讨会，围绕"大数据时代的反保险欺诈工作"主题，交流分享了两岸四地保险业应用大数据技术开展反保险欺诈的经验成果。在澳门签署内地与港澳三地保险监管部门反欺诈合作备忘录。初步建立保险业反洗钱制度机制，对4家保险机构进行反洗钱专项检查。发布《保险机构洗钱和恐怖融资风险评估及客户分类管理指引》，指导保险机构合理评估客户洗钱风险等级。组织行业完成非法集资案件排查工作，开展防范打击非法集资宣传月活动，发放宣传资料145万份，教育社会公众1 000多万人次。

保险法制体系建设

2014年，中国保监会不断加强和改进保险法制体系建设，目前已经形成由保险法、行政法规、行政规章、规范性文件四个层次构成的保险法制体系，为夯实行业发展基础，促进我国保险业持续、健康、快速发展发挥了重要作用。

完成《保险法》实施评估，推动《保险法》修改

2014年6月，中国保监会完成对《保险法》实施评估，确定了修改方向和重点。2014年7月，正式启动了保险法修改起草工作，2014年底就修改条文初稿向保险业内、部分专家学者征求了意见，对初稿内容作进一步的论证研究和梳理完善。

完善监管规章制度

2014年，中国保监会修改并发布了以下四部规章：
- 《保险公司董事、监事和高级管理人员任职资格管理规定》
- 《中国保险监督管理委员会行政许可实施办法》
- 《保险资金运用管理暂行办法》
- 《保险公司股权管理办法》

加强规范性文件管理

2014年上半年，中国保监会对现行有效的规范性文件进行了全面清理。根据"法制统一、顺应市场、精简高效"的原则，科学有序地推进规范性文件的立、改、废，有效提升了规范性文件体系的科学性、系统性。

对外合作交流

2014年，中国保监会不断加强与国际保险监督官协会（IAIS）、国际养老金监督官协会（IOPS）、亚洲开发银行（ADB）、扩大保险服务计划（A2ii）等国际组织的交流与合作，积极参与亚洲保险监督官论坛（AFIR）活动并担任轮值主席，继续巩固与重点国家（地区）的双边协作，探索开展跨境监管、养老保险、健康险、偿付能力和资金运用监管等专题合作。建立健全与美国、欧盟、加拿大、英国、法国、澳大利亚、泰国、马恩岛等国家（地区）保险监管机构的合作机制，继续大力支持港、澳、台地区金融业发展。广泛参与国际保险监管规则制定、国际保险交流活动和区域性平台建设。不断扩大保险业对外开放，配合国家整体对外工作战略，参与多个多双边磋商机制，促进了监管机构间的信息共享和技术交流，有效地防范了风险跨境、跨领域传递，为扩大中国保险业国际影响力，促进中国保险业持续健康稳定发展发挥了积极作用。

监管队伍与信息化建设

监管队伍

截至2014年底，中国保监会系统现有在职干部2 835人，其中会机关383人，派出机构2 452人；男性1 717人，占比61%，女性1 118人，占比39%；本科及以上学历2 813人，占比99%；45岁以下干部2 547人，占比90%。

2014年，中国保监会加大教育培训工作力度。制定印发《2014-2018年中国保监会干部教育培训规划》，举办3期局级领导干部学习贯彻习近平总书记系列重要讲话精神轮训班。

信息化建设

监管机制不断完善，监管手段创新突破

2014年，中国保监会重新组建了信息化工作领导小组，制定了领导小组工作规则，推动建立监管信息化治理架构和工作机制。进一步完善保险业标准化规范。推进《保险电子商务平台建设基本规范》《保险术语》等10项标准制修订工作。首次运用技术手段对10家保险公司进行了远程渗透性测试检查，研究建立信息化风险非现场监管和评价体系。

监管信息化建设取得新进展

2014年，中国保监会加强监管应用信息系统开发和升级，新建人事综合考评系统、中介市场清查系统等6个信息系统，改造升级电子文件传输系统等4个信息系统，监管信息化建设取得新进展。完成了南京异地灾备中心的规划设计及基建工作，就建设同城主数据中心开展了可行性研究，向构建"两地三中心"现代化保险基础架构体系迈出了坚实一步。

保险系统员工摄影作品

保险系统员工摄影作品

05

保险市场运行状况

- 财产保险市场情况
- 人身保险市场情况
- 保险中介市场情况
- 保险资金运用市场情况
- 专业再保险市场
- 保险业对外开放情况

2014年，中国保险业共实现保费收入20 233.6亿元，同比增长17.5%。保险深度为3.18%，保险密度为1 479.3元。赔款给付金额达7 194.4亿元，同比增长15.9%。保险公司总资产达10.2万亿元，较年初增长22.3%。

财产保险市场情况

保费收入平稳增长

2014年，财产保险公司实现保费收入7 546.1亿元，同比增长16.4%，增速较2013年同期下降0.8个百分点。其中车险保费收入5 515.9亿元，同比增长16.8%，非车险保费收入2 030.2亿元，同比增长15.3%。

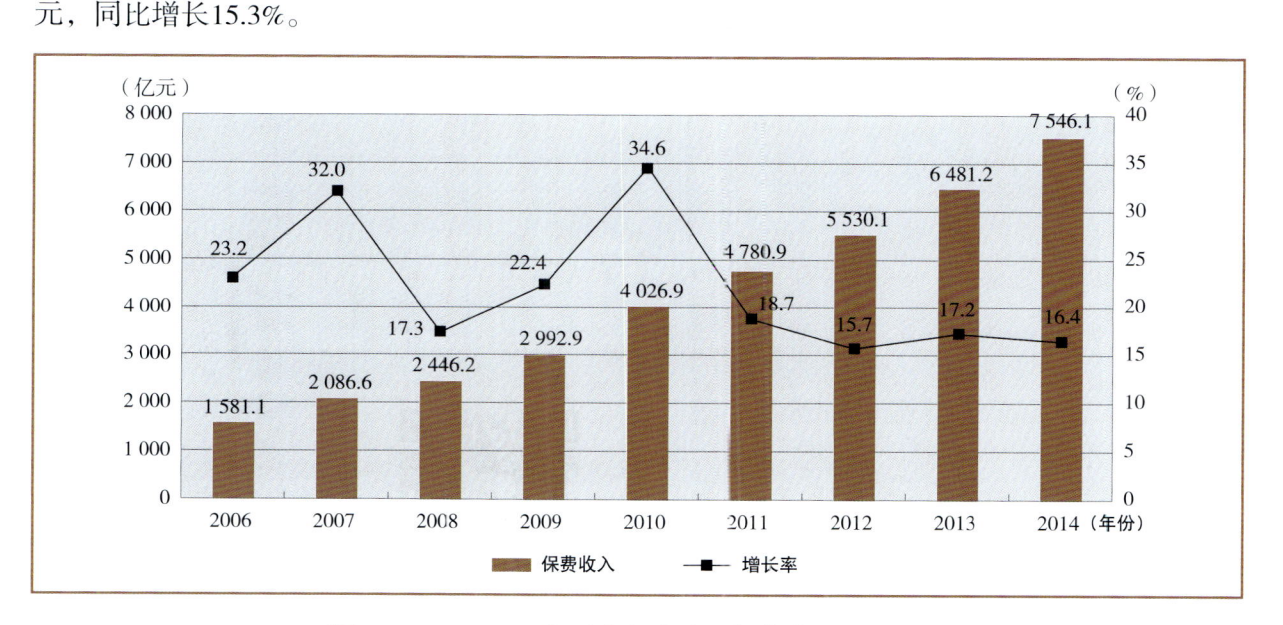

图1　2006—2014年财产保险公司保费收入及增长率

保费收入构成前5位的是车险、企财险、农业险、责任险和信用险，分别为5 515.9亿元、387.4亿元、325.8亿元、253.4亿元、200.7亿元，占全部保费收入的88.6%。

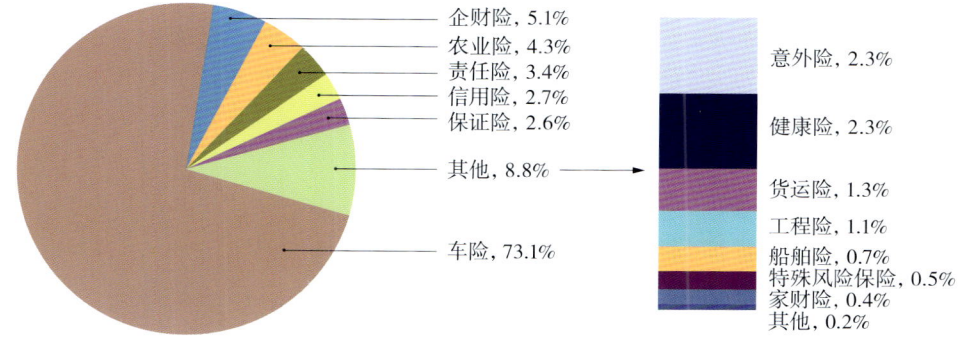

图2　2014年财产保险公司业务结构

财产保险公司多数险种实现稳步增长，其中车险、责任险、信用险、保证险、意外险、健康险分别增长16.8%、16.9%、29.3%、66.1%、14.1%、44.5%。

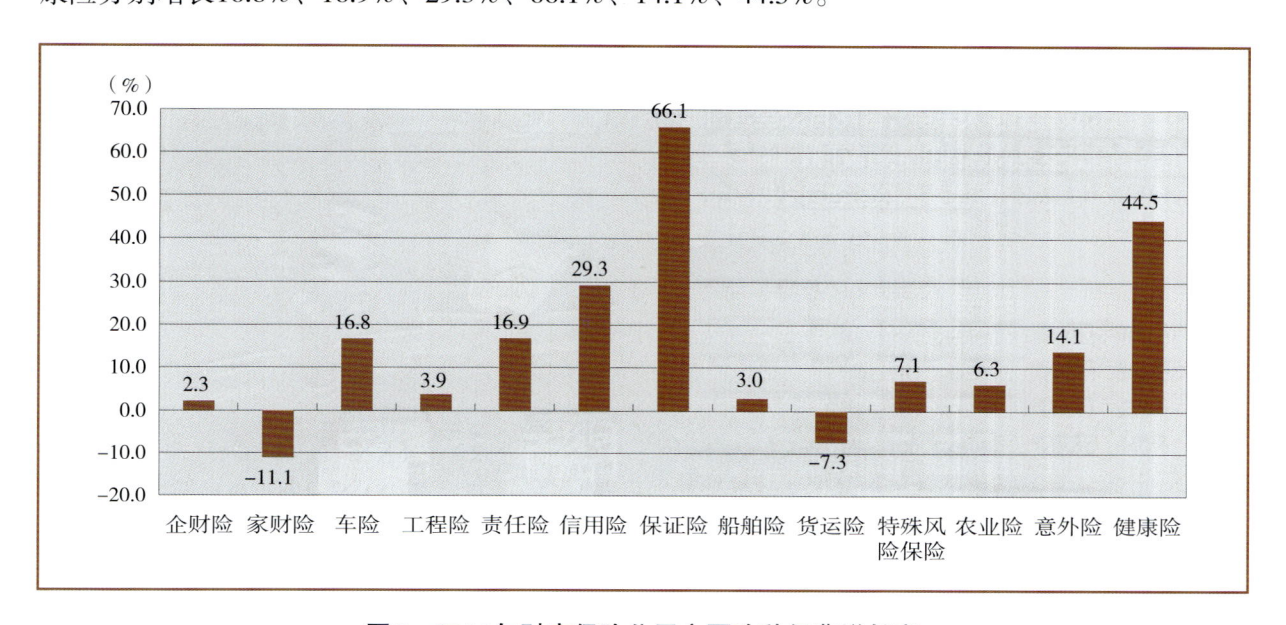

图3　2014年财产保险公司主要险种保费增长率

行业资本实力大幅增强

2014年，财产保险公司总资产合计1.4万亿元，同比增长26.9%，高于保费增速10.5个百分点；净资产合计3 840.6亿元，同比增长52.9%，高于保费增速36.5个百分点。

市场集中度有所上升

截至2014年末，全国共有财产保险公司67家，其中中资45家、外资22家。保费收入前5家公司市场份额共计74.7%，较上年同期上升0.4个百分点。

表1　2014年财产保险公司保费收入前十名

排名	公司名称	资本结构	保费（亿元）	市场份额（%）
1	中国人民财产保险股份有限公司	中资	2 524.2	33.4
2	中国平安财产保险股份有限公司	中资	1 428.6	18.9
3	中国太平洋财产保险股份有限公司	中资	928.4	12.3
4	中国人寿财产保险股份有限公司	中资	404.0	5.4
5	中华联合财产保险股份有限公司	中资	348.7	4.6
6	中国大地财产保险股份有限公司	中资	223.6	3.0
7	阳光财产保险股份有限公司	中资	211.7	2.8
8	中国出口信用保险公司	中资	181.2	2.4
9	太平财产保险有限公司	中资	132.7	1.8
10	天安财产保险股份有限公司	中资	111.5	1.5
	合计		6 494.6	86.1

承保盈利同比回升

2014年，财产保险公司实现承保利润42.6亿元，同比增长93.5%，其中车险承保亏损11.9亿元，实现减亏20.7亿元。受资金运用收益大幅上涨影响，行业实现净利润520.5亿元，同比增长94%。

行业风险可控

2014年底，各财产保险公司偿付能力和核心资本指标均达标，所有财险公司偿付能力充足率均高于150%，行业准备金较为充足，未出现系统性、区域性风险。

保障水平持续提升

2014年，财产保险公司承担风险金额761.7万亿元，是同期名义GDP总量的12倍，同比增长13%。全年行业共支付赔款3 969亿元，同比增长11.7%。财产保险公司积极参与重大灾害的抗灾、救灾工作，帮助受灾地区及时恢复生产生活，充分发挥改善民生保障、救灾减灾的作用。2014年，财险行业向辽宁特大旱灾的118.7万受灾农户支付赔款9.3亿元，向威马逊台风和海鸥台风影响的海南、广东、广西三省受灾群众支付赔款15.5亿元和4.2亿元。

人身保险市场情况

保费收入快速增长

2014年，人身保险市场发展势头强劲，人身保险公司全年实现保费收入12 687.3亿元，同比增长18.2%，增速较2013年提高10.3个百分点。截至2014年末，人身保险公司新单保费收入6 568.6亿元，同比增长31.5%，占人身保险公司总保费的51.8%。新单期交保费收入1 747.6亿元，同比增长18.9%，占人身保险公司新单保费收入的26.6%。

产品结构明显优化

受益于人身保险费率市场化改革，人身保险产品结构显著改善。2014年，普通寿险保费收入4 296.5亿元，同比增长258%，保费占比33.9%。分红保险保费收入6 508.8亿元，同比下降20%，保费占比51.3%。投连险保费收入4.4亿元，同比增长0.1%，保费占比0.03%。万能险保费收入91.9亿元，同比增长5%，保费占比0.7%。

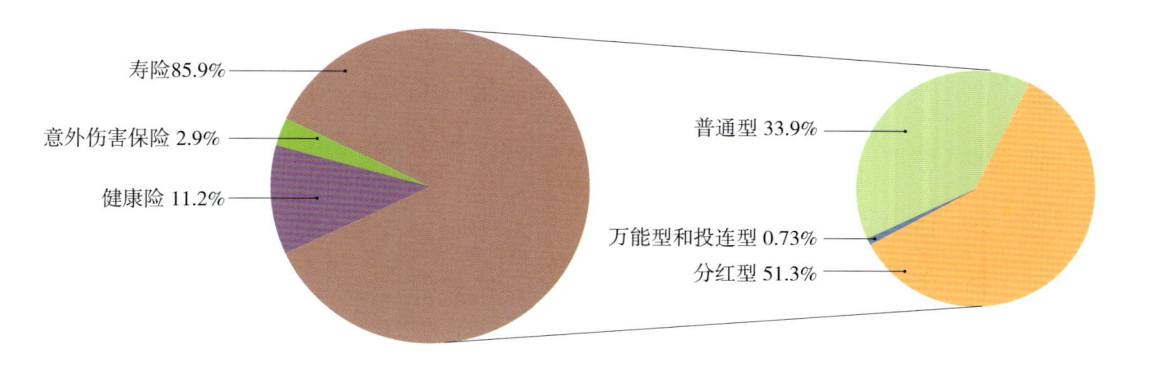

寿险85.9%

意外伤害保险 2.9%

健康险 11.2%

普通型 33.9%

万能型和投连型 0.73%

分红型 51.3%

图4 2014年人身保险公司业务构成

2014年，人身保险公司健康险和意外险保费收入增长迅速，健康险保费收入1 415.8亿元，同比增长41.6%，意外险保费收入370.7亿元，同比增长19.4%。健康险和意外险占总保费的14.1%，较2013年同期提高1.8个百分点。

专栏九 《人身保险伤残评定标准及代码》正式实施

2014年1月1日，《人身保险伤残评定标准及代码》正式实施。《人身保险伤残评定标准及代码》扩大了意外伤残保障范围，提升了意外险伤残理赔管理的规范性和标准化水平，同时为未来保险业意外险数据的规范、收集和分析奠定了基础，有助于推动意外险经营与管理的全面升级。

各渠道业务平稳发展

2014年，个人代理渠道保费收入6 174.5亿元，同比增长12.4%，保费占比48.6%，较2013年降低2.5个百分点。银保渠道保费收入4 946.9亿元，同比增长25.5%，保费占比39%，较2013年提高2.3个百分点。公司直销渠道保费收入1 264.7亿元，同比增长23.8%，保费占比10%，较2013年提高0.4个百分点。专业代理渠道保费收入74.9亿元，同比下降1.6%。其他兼业代理渠道保费收入163.4亿元，同比增长3.6%。保险经纪渠道保费收入62.8亿元，同比增长38.9%。

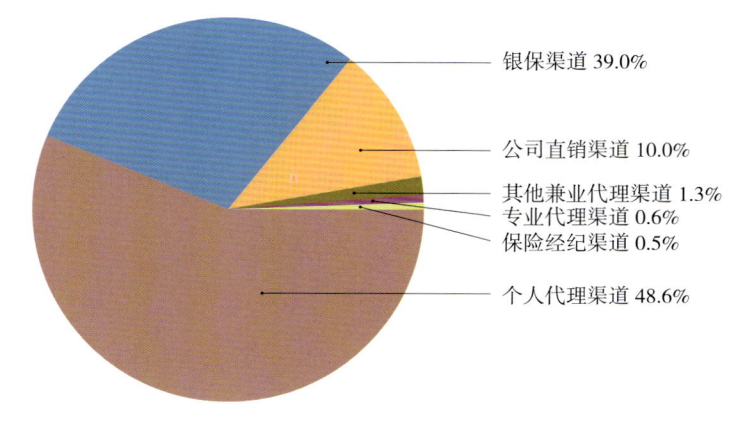

银保渠道 39.0%

公司直销渠道 10.0%

其他兼业代理渠道 1.3%
专业代理渠道 0.6%
保险经纪渠道 0.5%

个人代理渠道 48.6%

图5 2014年人身保险公司保费收入渠道构成

发展实力不断增强

截至2014年末，人身保险公司资产总额达82 545.4亿元，较2013年同期增长20.8%，实现利润总额1 092.7亿元，同比增长119.6%。偿付能力溢额大幅增长，资本缓冲垫进一步增厚。

截至2014年末，全国共有73家人身保险公司，较2013年增加3家。其中，中资公司45家，外资公司28家。

2014年，保费收入前五家人身保险公司市场份额合计为62.4%，较2013年降低7.1个百分点，市场集中度继续下降。

赔款与给付支出增长较快

2014年，人身保险公司各项赔款与给付支出3 225亿元，同比增长21.6%。

表2　2014年人身保险公司保费收入前十名

排名	公司名称	资本结构	保费（亿元）	市场份额（%）
1	中国人寿保险股份有限公司	中资	3 310.0	26.1
2	中国平安人寿保险股份有限公司	中资	1 739.9	13.7
3	新华人寿保险股份有限公司	中资	1 098.7	8.7
4	中国太平洋人寿保险股份有限公司	中资	986.9	7.8
5	中国人民人寿保险股份有限公司	中资	786.3	6.2
6	泰康人寿保险股份有限公司	中资	679.0	5.3
7	太平人寿保险有限公司	中资	651.3	5.1
8	安邦人寿保险股份有限公司	中资	528.9	4.2
9	生命人寿保险股份有限公司	中资	367.1	2.9
10	中邮人寿保险股份有限公司	中资	219.5	1.7
	合计		10 367.6	81.7

表3　2014年人身保险公司赔偿给付金额

险种	赔款给付金额（亿元）	同比增长（%）	占比（%）
寿险	2 704.8	20.2	83.9
健康险	446.9	33.3	13.8
意外险	73.2	11.9	2.3
合计	3 224.9	21.6	100.0

市场风险有效防范

一是平稳化解满期给付和退保风险。2014年，人身保险公司退保金额为3 230.9亿元，同比增长69.5%，退保率为5.71%。保险业不断加大风险防范力度，顺利度过满期给付和退保高

峰期，守住了风险底线。二是成功处置个别风险。妥善处置了风险爆发的个别公司风险，维护了行业整体稳定。三是偿付能力整体充足。2014年末，仅有一家人身保险公司偿付能力不达标，达标公司偿付能力充足率均在150%以上。四是规范了高现金价值业务发展。2014年初，针对高现金价值业务"井喷"式增长的态势，中国保监会及时出台调控政策，印发了《关于规范高现金价值产品有关事项的通知》，《通知》印发后的第二、第三和第四季度，高现金价值业务分别较第一季度大幅下降80%、85%、84%，遏制了"井喷"式发展势头。

保险中介市场情况

主体发展情况

保险专业中介机构

截至2014年末，全国共有保险专业中介机构2 546家，同比增加21 家。其中，保险专业代理机构1 764家，保险经纪机构445家，保险公估机构337家。全国保险专业中介机构注册资本261.6亿元，同比增长16.8%。

保险兼业代理机构

截至2014 年末，全国共有保险兼业代理机构网点210 108个，其中，金融类179 061个，非金融类31 047个。

市场运行情况

2014 年，全国保险公司通过保险中介渠道实现保费收入16 144.2亿元，占2014 年全国总保费收入的79.8%，同比下降0.5%。其中，财产险4 721.7亿元，人身险11 422.5亿元。

保险专业中介渠道

2014 年，保险专业中介渠道实现保费收入1 472.4亿元，占2014 年全国总保费收入的7.3%，同比增长28.2%。

——保险代理机构实现保费收入967.9亿元，占2014 年全国总保费收入的4.8%，其中财产险保费收入893亿元，人身险保费收入74.9亿元。佣金收入184.8亿元，其中财产险佣金收入156.6亿元，人身险佣金收入28.2亿元。

——保险经纪机构实现保费收入504.5亿元，占2014 年全国总保费收入的2.5%，其中财产险保费收入441.7亿元，人身险保费收入62.8亿元。业务收入94.2亿元，其中财产险业务收入71.9亿元，人身险业务收入11.6亿元，再保险业务收入1.8亿元，咨询业务收入8.9亿元。

——保险公估机构实现业务收入22.6亿元。

保险兼业代理渠道

2014 年，全国保险兼业代理渠道实现保费收入7 008.9亿元，占2014 年全国总保费收入的34.6%，其中财产险保费收入1 898.6亿元，人身险保费收入5 110.3亿元。

个人代理渠道

2014年，全国保险个人代理渠道实现保费收入7 662.9亿元，占2014 年全国总保费收入的37.9%，其中财产险保费收入1 488.4亿元，人身险保费收入6 174.5亿元。

保险资金运用市场情况

截至2014年末，保险资金运用余额为9.3万亿元，占保险业总资产的91.9%，较年初增加1.6万亿元，增幅为21.4%。

从配置结构看，一是固定收益类资产继续保持主导地位，国债、金融债和企业债等各类债券余额为3.6万亿元，在投资资产中占比38.2%；银行存款 2.5万亿元，占比27.1%。二是权益类资产稳中有升，投资股票和基金的余额为1万亿元，占比11.1%，较年初的10%增长1.1个百分点。三是另类投资增长较快，长期股权投资6 398.8亿元，占比6.9%；投资性不动产784.4亿元，占比0.8%；基础设施投资计划产品等7 317亿元，占比7.8%。长期股权投资、不动产投资、基础设施投资计划等分别比年初增长59%、13.9%和66%。

从投资收益看，2014年保险资金运用实现投资收益5 358.8亿元，较2013年增加1 700.5亿元；财务收益率为6.3%，同比提高1.3个百分点；综合收益率为9.2%，同比提高5.1个百分点。财务收益率和综合收益率均创近五年来最好水平。

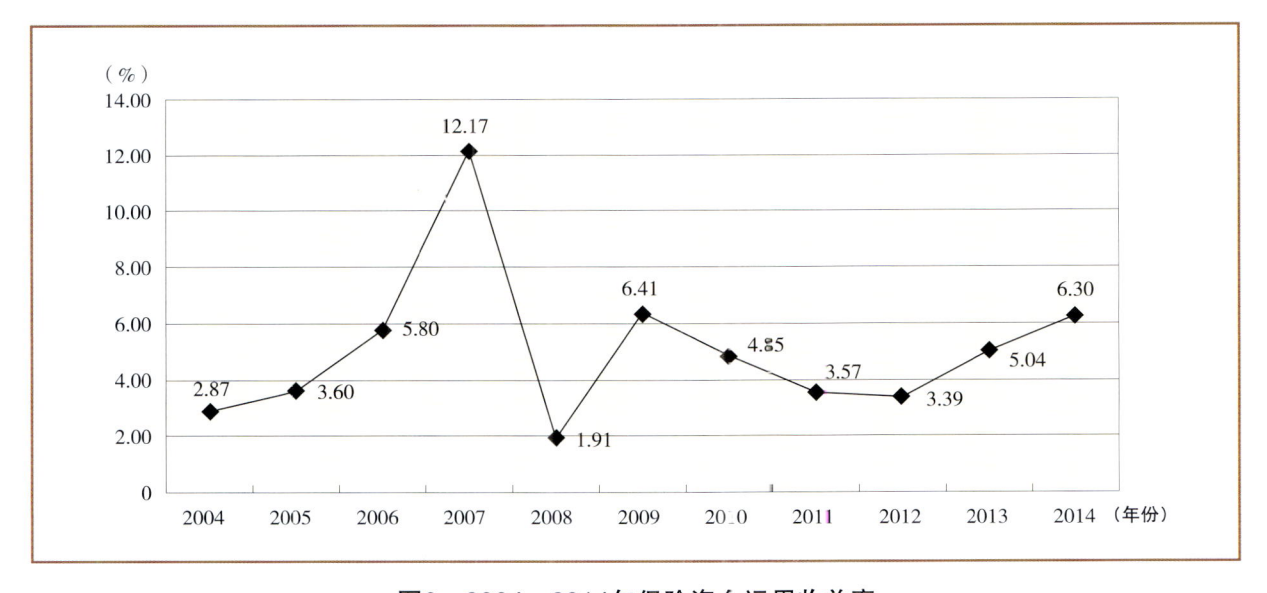

图6　2004—2014年保险资金运用收益率

专业再保险市场

直保公司再保险分出规模持续增长

2014年，直保公司总分出保费1 737.8亿元，同比增长52%。其中，产险公司总分出保费929.4亿元，同比增长7.7%。寿险公司总分出保费808.4亿元，同比增长188.6%。2014年，部分寿险公司为缓解偿付能力压力，大规模安排临时性再保险分出，是寿险公司总分出保费增长较快的主要原因。

再保险公司继续保持稳健发展

2014年，全国再保险公司的总分保费收入为1 518.5亿元，同比增长55.7%；总分保赔款支出393亿元，同比增长11.2%。2014年，全国再保险公司共实现承保利润11.7亿元，实现净利润58.8亿元。

拓展海外市场的步伐加快

2014年，跨境人民币结算再保险业务分保费收入为95.4亿元；经营主体发展到7家；业务来源扩展至香港、澳门、新加坡、台湾4个市场。

再保险市场扩容提速

截至2014年末，全国共有1家再保险（集团）公司和9家专业再保险公司。受新国十条和偿二代政策影响，2014年，多家大型保险企业有意设立专业再保险公司，多家离岸再保险公司积极谋求在境内设立分支机构，社会资本积极提出进入再保险领域。

保险业对外开放情况

外资保险公司在华经营情况

2014年，外资保险公司实现保费收入901.9亿元，同比增长32.6%，占全国保费收入的4.5%，占比较上年提高0.5个百分点。各类赔款与给付支出472亿元。外资保险公司总资产6 646.7亿元，较年初增加2 231.4亿元，增长50.5%，占保险业总资产的6.5%。

截至2014年底，共有15个国家和地区的保险公司在我国设立了56家外资保险公司，外国保险机构在华设立代表处140家。

表4　2014年北京、上海、广州、深圳外资保险发展情况

城市	外资保费收入（亿元）	同比增长（%）	外资财产保险公司		外资人身保险公司	
			保费收入（亿元）	同比增长（%）	保费收入（亿元）	同比增长（%）
北京	162.2	10.4	16.3	31.5	145.8	8.5
上海	143.8	14.6	26.8	36.0	117.0	10.5
广州	105.3	29.6	13.3	17.7	92.2	31.7
深圳	38.0	10.5	6.2	51.2	31.8	5.1

外资财产保险公司

2014年，外资财产保险公司保费收入为168亿元，同比增长102.4%，市场份额为2.2%。外资财产保险公司赔款支出91.2亿元，同比增长50.5%。

外资财产保险公司业务结构中，车险、企财险、责任险、货运险、农业保险、意外险构成了业务主要来源，上述六个险种占比分别为56.6%、11.5%、9.1%、7.3%、5.9%、4.7%，合计占比95.1%。

表5　外资财产保险公司保费收入前五名

序号	2014年		2013年		2012年	
	名称	在外资财产保险公司中占比（%）	名称	在外资财产保险公司中占比（%）	名称	在外资财产保险公司中占比（%）
1	安盛天平	39.4	中航安盟	17.2	美亚	16.4
2	中航安盟	8.7	美亚	13.8	利宝互助	10.7
3	美亚	7.0	利宝互助	10.2	安盟	10.5
4	史带财产	6.3	安联	7.9	安联	8.6
5	安联	5.3	三星	7.4	三星	7.7
	合计	66.7	合计	56.5	合计	53.9

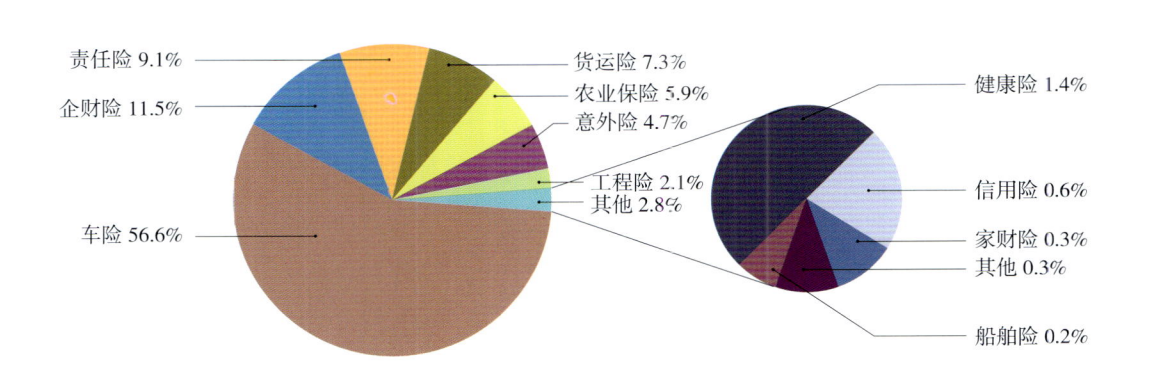

图7　外资财产保险公司业务构成

外资人身保险公司

2014年，外资人身保险公司实现保费收入733.9亿元，同比增长23%，市场份额为5.8%；外资人身保险公司各类赔付支出136.9亿元，同比增长60.2%。

表6　外资人身保险公司市场份额前五名

序号	2014年		2013年		2012年	
	名称	在外资人身保险公司中占比（%）	名称	在外资人身保险公司中占比（%）	名称	在外资人身保险公司中占比（%）
1	工银安盛	21.0	工银安盛	17.2	友邦	18.3
2	友邦	14.4	友邦	15.8	工银安盛	10.0
3	中美联泰	9.2	中美联泰	9.5	中美联泰	9.8
4	中意	7.6	中意	8.0	中意	8.8
5	招商信诺	7.2	招商信诺	7.1	信诚	7.6
	合计	59.4	合计	57.6	合计	54.5

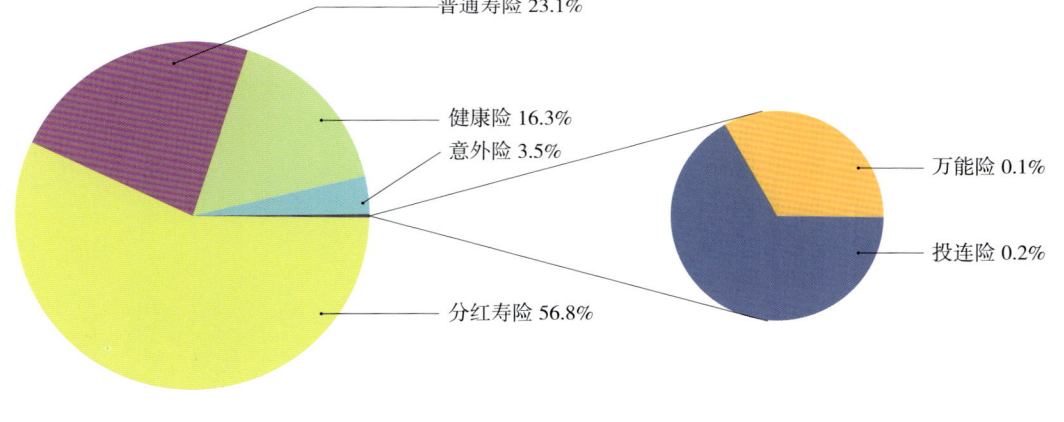

图8　外资人身保险公司业务构成

外资再保险公司

外资再保险公司实现分保费收入983.5亿元，同比增长104.1%，占全国再保险公司分保费收入的64.8%；总分保赔付支出227.5亿元，同比增长12%；利润总额18.2亿元，同比增长72.8%。

中资保险机构在海外设立机构情况

截至2014年末，共有12家境内保险机构在境外设立了32家营业机构，其中包括10家资产管理公司。共有4家境内保险机构在境外设立了7家代表处。

保险系统员工摄影作品

06

保险业改革创新

- 深入学习贯彻落实新国十条，开启保险业加快发展新纪元
- 保险业全面深化各项改革，行业市场化水平显著提升
- 保险业创新发展，行业市场活力明显增强

深入学习贯彻落实"新国十条",开启保险业加快发展新纪元

2014年8月,国务院发布了《关于加快发展现代保险服务业的若干意见》(以下简称"新国十条")。"新国十条"共10个方面,32项内容,主题鲜明、内涵丰富、重点突出、力度空前,就保险业的改革发展提出了一系列重大战略部署,对发展现代保险服务业意义重大。提升了保险业的行业定位,首次明确保险业是现代经济的重要产业,从国家治理体系和治理能力现代化的高度,对加快发展现代保险服务业作出了顶层设计。明确了战略目标,到2020年,使保险成为政府、企业、居民风险管理和财务管理的基本手段,保险深度达到5%、保险密度达到3500元/人。制定了统筹规划,对新时期保险业改革、发展和监管进行了全面部署,并明确要求完善保险法规体系,确保改革发展的规范进行。丰富了行业政策体系,提出税收政策、财政政策、用地保障政策等一系列系统性支持政策措施,将为保险业发展注入强大的动力和活力。

"新国十条"的发布实施是党中央、国务院站在历史和时代的高度,着眼于经济社会发展全局作出的重要战略部署,翻开了保险业加快发展和走向腾飞的新篇章,为新形势下做好监管工作提供了思想指针和行动指南。"新国十条"下发后,引起了国内外广泛反响,国际保险业对"新国十条"高度评价,认为中国对保险业在社会治理中作用的认识走在世界前列,"新国十条"是对国际保险理论和保险实践的重要贡献。

保险业把学习贯彻"新国十条"精神作为工作的重中之重。中国保监会专门制定了贯彻落实"新国十条"的工作方案,举办保险公司"一把手"学习贯彻"新国十条"培训班,开展"新国十条"的系统宣传,中国保监会领导亲赴各省进行宣讲。协会、学会、各局举办了各种形式的培训班,召开省市金融办负责人座谈会,推动各地出台贯彻落实"新国十条"的实施意见,协调相关部委按照任务分工落实支持政策。2014年,在中国保监会的积极推动下,保险业贯彻落实"新国十条"要求,各项工作亮点纷呈。

一是持续深化保险市场化改革。研究制订万能险费率改革方案,草拟开展商业车险费率市场化改革的指导意见,继续推动保险资金运用改革。市场化改革的推进有效地解放了行业生产力,激发了市场活力。

二是进一步完善保险市场体系。截至2014年底,全国共有保险法人机构187家,分支机构7.8万家,基本形成了综合性、专业性、区域性和集团化保险机构齐头并进,自保、相互、互联网等新型市场主体创新发展,统一开放、协调发展、充满活力的现代保险市场体系。

三是参与完善社会保障体系。保险业通过开展城乡居民大病保险工作、参与各类医疗保障项目经办管理、开发补充养老健康计划、参与管理企业年金和职业年金等,有效地弥补了社会养老医疗保障的不足。

四是积极服务现代农业。2014年,农业保险覆盖范围日益扩大,服务水平逐步提升。我国农险保费规模仅次于美国,居全球第二,养殖业保险和森林保险规模已跃居全球第一。

五是创新社会治理,健全灾害事故防范救助体系。发挥责任保险化解矛盾纠纷功能,大力发展食品安全、医疗卫生及环境保护等领域责任保险。探索建立巨灾保险制度,研究推动巨灾

保险立法，开展巨灾保险试点。

六是保护消费者利益。制定《中国保监会关于加强保险消费者权益保护工作的意见》，切实解决消费者关心的突出问题，发布《中国保监会关于2014年暨近三年财产保险积压未决赔案清理专项工作情况的通报》，使社会公众可以监督消费者利益保护的成效。

总的来看，贯彻落实"新国十条"开局良好，一批促进行业长远发展的政策正在出台，一系列关键领域的改革措施正在推出，各项创新制度接连涌现。各级政府十分重视，有21个省、市出台了促进现代保险服务业发展的文件，2个省、市即将印发，5个省、市的文件已经完成征求意见工作。

当前，保险业站在了新的历史起点上，下一步全行业将坚持服务全局，坚持市场主导，坚持底线思维，拓展行业发展空间，发挥行业功能作用，切实服务经济社会发展，全面贯彻落实"新国十条"要求。可以预计，在党中央、国务院的关心指导下，在行业全体从业人员的辛勤努力下，保险业的发展必将迎来更加美好的明天。

浙江省出台"新国十条"贯彻落实意见

2014年9月2日，浙江省政府出台《关于进一步发挥保险功能作用促进我省经济社会发展的意见》，成为全国首个出台"新国十条"实施意见的省份。《意见》提出了落实"新国十条"、推进保险服务浙江发展的十个方面举措，明确小额贷款保证保险、巨灾保险等17项重点政保合作项目和相应19个责任部门。浙江保监局联合省金融办，通过举办"浙江省保险支持地方经济社会发展推进会"、建立全省保险专家库制度、召开现场经验交流会等方式，鼓励各级政府通过委托保险机构经办或直接购买保险产品和服务等方式为公众提供更高效率的公共服务，积极推进政保合作项目试点扩面。

专栏十　农产品目标价格保险试点成效显著

2014年，中国保监会认真贯彻落实中央一号文件和"新国十条"精神要求，大力推进目标价格保险试点，取得较好成效。全年已有20个省市启动或制定了目标价格保险试点方案。其中，黑龙江、河北、河南等15个省市已签发保单；山东、辽宁等5省已制定工作方案并开发出保险产品，拟于2015年启动。2014年，目标价格保险参保农户77万户次，保费收入2.8亿元，提供风险保障62亿元，是保费的22倍。主要险种包括粮食作物目标价格保险、生猪目标价格保险、蔬菜目标价格保险、地方特色农产品目标价格保险等。

专栏十一　北京保险产业园建设驶入快车道

2014年4月8日，北京保险产业园创新发展座谈会暨揭牌仪式在石景山区召开。中国保监会主席项俊波、北京市市委副书记、市长王安顺共同为北京保险产业园揭牌，保险产业园建设驶入快车道。该产业园建设的总体目标是打造以保险产业为龙头的国家级金融创新示范区，通过创造良好环境、提供优质服务，努力将北京保险产业园建设成为全国保险创新试验区、保险产业聚集区和保险文化引领区，重点吸引保险业改革创新的增量。

中国保险信息技术管理有限责任公司成立	**"新方位·新机遇·新未来——保险强国之路"学术年会成功举办**

2014年1月15日，中国保险信息技术管理有限责任公司正式成立。公司将以支持行业发展、服务保险监管、保护保险消费者为使命，以建设和运营集中统一、设计科学、功能完善、安全高效的保险业数据信息共享和对外交互平台为主要职责，积极探究保险行业信息交互共享需求。

中国首家海洋特色保险公司获准开业

2014年12月4日，华海财产保险股份有限公司正式获得中国保监会开业批复。华海财险是全国首家以海洋保险、互联网保险为特色的全国性、综合性、全民营财产保险公司，致力于为海洋产业、海岸经济和沿海地区提供专业化的综合保险服务。

2014年11月20日至21日，中国保险学会在京召开主题为"新方位·新机遇·新未来——保险强国之路"学术年会，围绕"新国十条"核心内容，开展深入研讨。项俊波主席出席会议并发表重要讲话，著名经济学家厉以宁出席会议并作"新常态和保险业"为题的主旨演讲，国际保险学会主席迈克尔·莫里西应邀参加会议并演讲。年会设主会场和八个专题会场，来自中央和国家机关相关部门、海内外保险机构的800余位代表参会。

保险业全面深化各项改革，行业市场化水平显著提升

稳步推进保险费率形成机制改革

人身险费率市场化改革

经国务院批准同意，中国保监会于2013年8月5日启动了人身险费率市场化改革，建立起了符合社会主义市场经济规律的费率形成机制，明确了"普通型、万能型、分红型人身险"分三步走的改革路径。2013年，普通型人身险费率市场化改革正式实施，取消了普通型人身险产品2.5%预定利率上限，明确准备金评估利率，降低保障产品资本要求。2014年，中国保监会积极推动万能险费率市场化改革工作。一是通过持续跟踪、总结普通型人身险费率政策改革，为深化万能险费率改革提供指导。二是在人身险费率形成机制改革整体框架下，推动万能险费率政策改革，完成精算规定的配套修订。三是充分论证并不断修改完善改革方案，综合平衡改革创新与风险控制、放开前端与管住后端的关系。按照工作计划，2015年初将正式放开万能险最低保证利率，争取年底放开分红险预定利率，实现人身险费率全面市场化。

普通型人身险预定利率放开以来，政策实施平稳，社会反响良好，风险有效控制，改革成效明显。一是产品供给丰富。自2013年8月5日改革以来至2014年年底，各人身险公司备案、审批的普通型人身险费率改革产品达675个，占同期报备普通型人身险产品的23.4%，产品的增加满足了消费者的需求。二是产品价格回落。改革后普通型人身险主流产品价格平均下降20%左右，消费者从改革中切实得到了实惠。三是业务快速增长。2014年，普通寿险业务保费收入

达4 296.5亿元，同比增长258%，占人身险保费收入33.9%，超过改革前约24个百分点，成为人身险业务发展的重要支柱之一。四是风险有效防范。行业没有出现因费率改革而引发的集中退保、恶性价格竞争等风险，新老产品平稳过渡。

商业车险改革

2014年，中国保监会正式启动商业车险改革。一是明确商业车险改革总体框架。拟定《关于深化商业车险条款费率管理制度改革的意见》，明确商业车险改革的总体目标、基本原则、主要内容和工作安排。二是做好商业车险改革配套工作。指导行业协会修订商业车险示范条款及配套单证，着力解决社会反映突出的问题。建立机动车车型名称标准，组织编制全国16万个车型的"身份证"，形成保险业独有的车型识别编码体系。研究建立创新型条款评估和保护机制，提高创新的有效性，增强创新动力。三是完成商业车险改革费率测算。构建费率测算框架体系，提高费率测算的科学性。组织对6.2亿条商业车险数据进行多维度的测算，建立首个车险精算数据库。制订多套费率测算方案，形成商业车险改革费率测算报告。完成商业车险纯保费测算工作，实现车险定价的重大突破。

偿付能力监管制度体系改革

2014年，中国保监会顺利完成第二代偿付能力监管制度体系三个支柱17项技术标准的制定和送审工作。一是完成第一支柱实际资本、最低资本、寿险合同负债评估等9项监管规则的制定，建立了风险导向的保险公司量化资本计量标准。二是完成第二支柱分类监管（风险综合评级）规则、偿付能力风险管理要求与评估规则、流动性风险监管规则的制定。三是完成第三支柱技术标准的制定，建立了偿付能力信息季度公开披露制度、监管部门与相关方之间的交流机制以及保险公司的信用评级制度。四是制定了保险集团偿付能力监管规则，首次将非保险机构控制的混合保险集团纳入监管范围，明确了保险集团的定量资本标准、偿付能力风险管理要求等。五是制定偿付能力报告监管规则，建立了以季报为核心的偿付能力报告体系。六是根据偿二代整体框架和技术标准制定情况，对《保险法》偿付能力相关条款提出了修改意见。

专栏十二　第二代偿付能力监管制度体系的技术框架

第二代偿付能力监管制度体系在我国保险业风险分层模型基础上，构建了审慎监管的三支柱框架。第一支柱定量监管要求，主要防范能够用资本量化的保险风险、市场风险、信用风险三大类可量化风险，要求保险公司具备与以上风险暴露相适应的资本。第二支柱定性监管要求，防范操作风险、战略风险、声誉风险和流动性风险四大类难以量化为资本要求的风险，并对保险公司风险管理能力进行评估。第三支柱市场约束机制，通过公开信息披露、提高透明度等手段，发挥市场的监督约束作用，防范依靠常规监管工具难以防范的风险。偿二代还建立了保险集团偿付能力监管的新框架，首次将非保险机构控制的混合保险集团纳入监管范围，加大了对集团一系列复杂风险的监管力度。

专栏十三　第二代偿付能力监管制度体系的影响

第二代偿付能力监管制度体系的建成和顺利实施，是中国保险监管改革和保险业发展历史上的重要里程碑，将加快我国保险监管体系现代化进程，支撑我国保险业持续健康快速发展，并对全球保险业竞争格局产生持久和重要的影响。

一是推动行业转变发展方式。偿二代全面科学计量保险公司的各种经营活动风险，强化了偿付能力监管对公司经营的刚性约束，督促保险公司在追求发展指标的同时，必须平衡考虑风险和资本成本，推动公司转变粗放的发展方式。

二是提升行业风险管理能力。偿二代建立了风险管理的经济激励机制，定期评估保险公司的风险管理能力，将风险管理能力直接反映到资本要求中，督促保险公司不断提高风险管理能力，进而提升行业核心竞争力。

三是增强保险业对资本的吸引力。偿二代释放了偿一代下过于保守的资本冗余，有利于提升保险公司的资本使用效率，增强保险业对社会资本的吸引力。

四是促进行业参与国际保险合作与交流。偿二代无论在"三支柱"监管框架，还是具体的监管标准和监管要求方面，与国际主流监管模式都是可比的，这为行业参与国际交流与合作提供了便利。

不断深化保险资金运用市场化改革

2014年，中国保监会不断深化保险资金运用市场化改革，切实简政放权，陆续发布12项政策制度，把更多投资选择权和风险责任交还给市场主体，激发了市场活力和创新动力，释放了改革红利。一是稳步拓宽投资范围。陆续发布一系列政策，放开保险资金投资创业板、历史存量保单投资蓝筹股、优先股、创业投资基金等。二是推行比例监管新模式。建立了以大类资产分类为基础，多层次的比例监管新体系，大大减少了比例限制，基本做到一个文件管比例。三是深化注册制改革。注册制改革大大提升了产品发行效率。截至2014年末，产品注册规模已达10 644.4亿元，与之前的备案规模2 941亿元相比，两年来注册规模已经是过去七年的3.5倍。四是强化事中事后监管。不断强化信息披露、内部控制、分类监管、资产托管、资产认可等监管工具，初步构建起"一个基础、五个工具和三个支撑"的现代化多层次监管框架。

专栏十四　中国保监会发布《关于加强和改进保险资金运用比例监管的通知》

2014年2月，中国保监会印发《关于加强和改进保险资金运用比例监管的通知》，整合了现行监管比例政策，建立了以保险资产分类为基础，多层次比例监管为手段，差异化监管为补充，动态调整机制为保障的比例监管新体系。《通知》的发布与实施，基本做到"一个文件管比例"。一方面，大大简化了监管比例，实现我国保险资金运用比例监管政策与国际监管惯例的初步接轨；另一方面，增强了市场活力，提高了监管效率，体现了"放开前端、管住后端"的监管思路及大力推进监管转型的基本取向。

专栏十五　保险资金运用领域2014年新规范一览

◆ 中国保监会关于保险资金投资创业投资基金有关事项的通知

◆ 中国保监会办公厅关于保险资金运用属地监管试点工作有关事项的通知

◆ 中国保监会　中国银监会关于规范保险资产托管业务的通知

◆ 中国保监会关于试行《保险资产风险五级分类指引》的通知

◆ 中国保监会关于保险资金投资优先股有关事项的通知

◆ 中国保监会关于印发《保险资金运用内控与合规计分监管规则》的通知

◆ 中国保监会关于印发《保险公司资金运用信息披露准则第1号：关联交易》的通知

◆ 关于保险资金投资集合资金信托计划有关事项的通知

◆ 关于授权北京等保监局开展保险资金运用监管试点工作的通知

◆ 中国保监会关于规范保险资金银行存款业务的通知

◆ 中国保监会关于加强和改进保险资金运用比例监管的通知

◆ 中国保监会关于保险资金投资创业板上市公司股票等有关问题的通知

专栏十六　中国保险资产管理业协会成立

2014年9月4日，中国保险资产管理业协会成立大会暨第一次会员代表大会在北京召开。保险资管协会是保险业市场化改革的重要成果，是保险资产管理监管方式转变的重要体制创新。作为市场主体和监管部门之间的桥梁和纽带，资管协会将履行维权、服务、创新、自律四大职能，以建设市场化、专业化、现代化、国际化的金融自律组织为目标，致力于成为提升行业能力、引导行业创新、推动行业发展的重要力量。

进一步完善市场准入退出制度

2014年，中国保监会按照"放开前端、管住后端"的思路，进一步健全市场准入退出机制。坚持市场化导向，突出专业化特色，正确把握发展与监管、监管与服务、维护投资者热情与保护消费者利益等重大关系，统筹规划市场准入和市场体系培育，完善市场退出和风险处置的制度机制，积极推动建立适度竞争、充满活力的保险市场体系。

一是正式出台《保险公司收购合并管理办法》。针对保险公司收购合并活动规定了多方面的鼓励政策和监管措施，充分发挥市场机制的决定性作用。二是坚持和完善新设保险公司逐步拓展经营区域制度。引导新设保险公司开业两年内首先在省域保险市场打牢基础、积累经验。三是扶持创新型主体发展。积极推进专业网络保险公司试点，扩大自保公司和保险互助社试点，鼓励公司走专业化和差异化发展道路，更好地服务经济社会发展。四是优化中资保险法人机构准入审核委员会制度。完善中资保险法人机构准入审核委员会的主要职责、审核对象和组织架构，增加审核委员，不断提高中资保险法人机构准入审核工作的质量和透明度。

专栏十七 《保险公司收购合并管理办法》出台

2014年3月，为进一步贯彻落实党的十八届三中全会精神、发挥市场机制对保险资源配置决定性作用，规范保险公司收购合并行为，促进保险市场资源的优化配置，中国保监会出台了《保险公司收购合并管理办法》。一是适度放宽资金来源，二是适度放宽股东资质，三是不再禁止同业收购。《保险公司收购合并管理办法》充分尊重商业自愿和引导市场自律，从信息披露、设定收购过渡期和股权锁定期、惩戒机制三个方面制定适度的监管措施。

专栏十八 我国互联网保险实现快速发展

2014年，我国互联网保险发展迅速、势头强劲。经营互联网保险的保险公司共94家，实现保费收入870.8亿元，较2013年增长1.7倍。互联网保险的发展模式主要包括保险公司直销、保险经纪代理、借助第三方平台和专业互联网保险公司模式。在多种发展模式下，全年互联网保险呈现出诸多亮点。如2014年"双十一"网购节，退货运费险单日成交超1.87亿单，保费收入超亿元，创造了保险业单日同一险种成交比数的世界纪录。首家专业互联网保险试点公司众安在线，2014年开发了近50款保险产品，实现保费收入近8亿元，提供风险保额19.4亿元，开业首年即实现盈利。在互联网保险监管方面，中国保监会坚持促进与规范并重的原则，积极引导互联网保险健康规范发展，研究起草了《互联网保险业务监管暂行办法》，以保护消费者权益和防范风险为重点，在信息披露、服务质量、信息安全等方面明确监管要求，强化市场退出管理，管住后端、守住底线。

深入推进保险产品监管改革

一是改进监管方式。拟定加强产品管理新规，完善规则，简政放权，强化公司主体责任。启动《财产保险公司保险条款和保险费率管理办法》修订进程，进一步研究完善产品监管制度，夯实产品监管基础。印发《关于规范财产保险公司保险产品开发销售有关问题的紧急通知》，规范保险产品开发、命名、销售、宣传等一系列环节的合法合规性操作，进一步保护了保险消费者的合法权益。二是改进监管手段。开展人身保险产品条款编码工作，推动中国保险行业协会建立行业人身保险产品数据库并投入使用，公众可通过扫描二维码或登录中保办网站查询条款，不断提高透明度。建设产品管理系统，推进信息化监管。三是推进基础工作。指导中国保险行业协会持续推进人身保险产品通俗化、简单化、标准化工作，开展意外险国际经验研究和示范条款修订；指导中国精算师协会组织相关专家开展现金价值课题研究等。

努力提升保险行业在汽车产业链中的地位

保险业积极参与汽车后市场体系建设。2014年9月，中国保监会与交通运输部、国家发展改革委等9部委共同印发《关于促进汽车维修业转型升级 提升服务质量的指导意见》，共同研究制订"建立汽车可追溯配件体系"工作方案，努力改善车险行业生态环境。

2014年，在中国保监会的指导下，中国保险行业协会联合中国汽车维修行业协会开展汽车配件"零整比"系数研究和发布工作，引导公众理性消费，正确认识车辆售后成本。国内常见汽车车型"零整比"研究成果，披露了36种常见车型的"整车配件零整比"和"50项易损配件零整比"系数。零整比研究成果的发布，产生了一系列积极效果：一是得到社会公众普遍认可。"零整比"系数首次公布后，10天之内网络曝光度超过一百万次。二是推动汽车行业反垄断工作深入开展。"零整比"研究成果直接推动了国家发展改革委等部门开展多项针对汽车纵向垄断行为的调查。三是对遏制零配件价格无序上涨发挥了积极作用，极大地提升了消费者对汽车维修的知情权和选择权，有效地提升了保险行业在汽车产业链中的地位。

专栏十九　我国汽车"零整比"特点

中国保险行业协会发布的国内常见汽车车型"零整比"研究成果表明，我国汽车"零整比"具有以下特点：一是"零整比"系数普遍偏高。据了解，国外汽车"零整比"一般在300%以内，但在已研究的国内36个车型中，"零整比"系数超过300%的有30个，占比为83%。二是不同车型间"零整比"系数差距较大。在36个车型中，"零整比"系数最高与最低车型的系数相差超过4倍。

保险业创新发展，行业市场活力明显增强

2014年，保险业以改革创新为动力，开拓新思路、提供新服务、建立新机制、探索新体制，市场活力不断激发，服务领域日益拓宽，竞争实力显著增强。

产品创新

2014年，保险机构着眼于保险产品的专业化和多样化，深耕保险市场，科学运用专业技术研发创新产品，寻找新的业务增长点，服务领域和范围进一步拓展。

阳光产险推出盗刷险　全面保障消费者账户安全

2014年，阳光产险正式推出"阳光盗刷险"，为消费者存折、存单、银行借记卡、银行信用卡主卡及附属卡、网银账户、手机银行账户、第三方支付账户等提供全面风险保障，解决一人持有多种账户管理复杂和安全隐患分散的问题。

富德生命人寿推出移动互联网年金保险

2014年，富德生命人寿推出移动互联网年金产品"宝贝存钱罐"，该产品为少儿年金保险，设计简单、有趣、个性化，投保方便灵活，家长可以随时将零散的小钱存入手机存钱罐，为孩子的未来做准备。

永诚保险成功承保光伏电站日照指数保险项目

2014年11月，永诚保险与瑞士再保险合作，成功承保三家光电集团光伏电站日照指数保险项目。该产品能够有效地转嫁太阳能光伏电站营运期发电量损失的风险，从而确保光伏电站的预期收益，同时，有助于光伏电站项目的融资增信。

浙商保险开展私募债保证保险业务

浙商保险与浙江股交中心、阿里巴巴合作，开展私募债保证保险业务。该创新产品为中小企业提供融资保障4亿多元，为中小型企业成功搭建成本较低、透明度较高的融资平台和渠道，帮助其降低融资成本，加快融资速度。

中国大地保险承保血站供血责任保险

2014年2月，中国大地保险重庆分公司承保重庆市血液中心血站供血责任保险项目，为年30万袋血浆的使用安全提供风险保障，有效地化解了受血者因输血致病、感染的潜在风险，保障社会公共卫生安全。

服务创新

2014年，保险业不断加强服务创新，持续完善保险服务体系。借助移动及互联网技术提高承保、查勘、定损及理赔效率，进一步提升客户满意度。

广东保险业有效提升小额信贷保证保险服务水平

广东保险业大力推动小额信贷保证保险工作，在江门市成立小微企业贷款保证保险服务中心，服务中心由江门市保险行业协会管理，保险公司负责日常运营，合作银行提供必要协助，面向小微企业提供无抵押贷款。借款企业融资成本由保证保险保费、银行贷款利息组成。从借款企业提供保单到贷款发放不超过5个工作日。该服务中心是保险业支持小微企业发展，服务地方经济转型升级的新尝试，形成了"政府支持，行业主导，企业认可"的良好局面。

中国人寿制定《理赔重大灾情应急管理办法》

为提升重大突发事件处理效率，提高服务水平，中国人寿制定《理赔重大灾情应急管理办法》，对重大灾情进行分级，明确应急预案、理赔服务、信息报告和其他事项。在2014年发生的马航MH370、云南鲁甸地震、江苏昆山爆炸、西藏尼木重大车祸等19件重大突发事件中，中国人寿快速反应，受到客户好评。

华泰人寿推出满期给付电话处理项目

2014年，华泰人寿推出满期给付电话处理项目，快速便捷的办理给付手续。截至2014年末，作为试点的上海分公司通过电话办理满期给付业务比例已占应处理业务的57%。

天安财险推出"车易赔"车险移动视频查勘系统

2014年，天安财险推出"车易赔"车险移动视频查勘系统，客户通过手机客户端应用无线网络技术进行前后台视频实时连线，对事故现场全程视频监控，同步完成查勘、定损、报价、核损、理算、核赔直至赔款支付的所有理赔环节，最快理赔时效达16分钟，有效地提升了车险理赔的便捷性。

管理创新

2014年，保险机构通过不断完善管理机制、创新管理技术、优化管理模式，提高企业运营效率，降低管理成本，增强核心竞争力。

福建投保人记录系统上线运行

2014年，福建投保人记录系统上线运行。该系统由保险销售人员通过个人智能手机下载客户端，在销售中按系统要求对投保人签名、抄录风险提示等关键环节进行拍照，并将照片上传专用平台，强化承保环节管控。该系统填补了保险销售过程中影像采集的空白，有助于提高保险销售的真实性，遏制代签名、代抄录行为，也为投保人信息大数据应用奠定了基础。

烟台保监分局推行"访后付费"制度

2014年，烟台保监分局在辖内首推"访后付费"制度，要求人身险公司在对承保一年期以上保单电话回访成功且投保人无疑问后，再向银邮类保险兼业代理机构支付手续费，着力解决银保渠道客户信息真实性差、有效电话回访成功率低等问题。该制度推行以来，辖内人身险公司客户信息真实性及回访成功率显著提高，保险消费者合法权益得到有效保护。

长江财险建立《管理逻辑表手册》

长江财险采用模块管理的方式，对各业务流程实行作业车间化、效率成本化、内控体检化的流程控制体系，形成了真正具有逻辑性、系统性的企业组织内专业条线的管理体系架构——《管理逻辑表手册》。首批管理逻辑表手册共计四册：《再保险分册》、《合规法务分册》、《监察审计分册》、《理赔客服分册》，为长江财险实现直接经济效益2 303万元，显著提升了服务效能，优化了合规指标达成度，培育了和谐企业文化。

机制、体制创新

2014年，保险业以全面深化改革为突破口，进一步加强经营管控、业务发展等制度机制建设，加快转变发展方式。

北京地区实施人身保险销售资质分类管理制度

2014年，北京保险业建立人身保险销售资质分类管理制度，针对新型寿险产品设立了两类销售资质：一是分红险、万能险销售资质，二是投连险、变额年金保险销售资质。要求在京寿险公司和在京开展寿险业务的各专业保险代理机构的销售从业人员在销售上述四类产品时，除必须持有《保险销售从业人员资格证书》外，还需要考取相应的销售资质，该制度计划在2015年7月1日起正式实施。销售分类资质管理制度将切实提高保险从业人员的专业性，进一步防范销售误导风险。

太平人寿开通FTE账户 探索跨境保险业务模式

2014年8月21日，太平人寿上海自贸试验区分公司开通自由贸易账户（FTE账户），实现外币保单境内销售和人民币保单境外销售，并以自由贸易账户为通道，通过再保分出分入及投资运作的形式，实现本外币保费资金双向跨境流通，使资产配置效能最大化。

平安人寿创新推出客户经理制

2014年，平安人寿电话销售渠道创新实施客户经理制，打通网电移一体化，对客户经理的留存、客户维护与服务都起到了积极作用，客户经理月均脱落率较非客户经理改善超30%。

技术创新

2014年，保险业积极以互联网技术为基础，运用大数据、云计算、移动通信等手段，提高风险数据与其他相关数据分析能力，为保险行业创新发展提供有效支持。

机动车辆保险信息平台实现全国统一集中管理

2014年5月，中国保险信息技术管理有限公司完成了对全国各地区车险平台的零故障安全迁移集中与切换，实现了车险平台的全国统一集中管理。车险平台的集中管理消除了以往各平台间的数据共享壁垒，实现了全国范围内机动车辆保险数据信息的汇集利用和交互共享。未来将通过系统重构和升级换代，在车险保费定价、车船税联网征收、代位求偿、反欺诈等方面发挥重要作用。

江苏率先建立交通与保险信息共享协作机制

2014年12月，江苏保监局与江苏省公安厅签订交通管理和保险服务信息化战略合作协议，建立机动车、驾驶人、交通违法信息、道路交通事故与车险基础信息数据共享机制。通过信息共享，可以有效地提升行业风险甄别水平和风险管理能力。

中国太保设立移动应用实验室

2014年6月，中国太保设立移动应用实验室。作为开放式的移动应用研发基地，实验室负责新技术收集、跟踪、应用研发、孵化和测试，将成为移动应用研发成果体验和企业品牌传播的载体。

安华农险成功研发植入式电子标签注射器

2014年，安华农险成功研发出第三代植入式电子标签注射器，将写入承保人、承保时间、身份识别码等信息的电子标签注射至生猪体内，可有效地解决养殖业保险承保标的不清的问题。理赔时将死因等信息写入电子标签并植入病死猪体内，能够有效地解决"病猪入市"问题。

中煤保险绘制并发布《中国煤矿风险地图》

2014年12月，中煤保险发布《中国煤矿风险地图》，该地图对全国煤矿的安全条件进行了综合评价，选取瓦斯等级、水文地质类型、煤尘爆炸性、煤层自燃倾向性、冲击地压共五个指标，采用AHP层次分析法建立评价模型，将安全条件按优、良、中、差分为A、B、C、D四个等级。在安全条件评价的基础上，结合全国煤矿安全质量化标准体系，从物的不安全状态和人的不安全行为两个维度，进一步建立客户风险等级评级体系，便于按客户风险等级情况制定核保方案，同时，可更有针对性地为煤炭企业提供风险预防、灾害补偿等增值服务。

保险系统员工摄影作品

保险系统员工摄影作品

07

保险消费者权益保护与教育

- 加强保险消费者权益保护顶层制度建设
- 及时化解保险消费纠纷
- 切实解决保险消费者关心的突出问题
- 加强与保险消费者有关信息披露
- 扎实开展保险消费者教育工作

加强保险消费者权益保护顶层制度建设

2014年，中国保监会在借鉴国际保险监管组织消费者保护原则和国际金融保险消费者权益保护良好经验、立足我国保险消费者权益保护工作实际的基础上制定了《中国保监会关于加强保险消费者权益保护工作的意见》，明确了当前和今后一个时期保险消费者权益保护工作的指导思想、基本原则和工作目标，提出了加强保险消费者权益保护工作的主要任务、政策取向和保障措施。制定并与国家发展改革委联合发布《中国保险业信用体系建设规划（2015－2020年）》。该《规划》立足于我国保险业信用体系建设实际，明确了未来5年保险业信用体系建设的目标任务，是我国首个行业性信用体系建设规划，也是保险业取信社会、取信消费者的"行动纲领"。

及时化解保险消费纠纷

2014年，中国保监会加强12378保险消费者投诉维权热线建设，在未设立热线分中心的22个保监局全面设立分中心，建成覆盖所有保监局的12378服务网络体系，实现"本地接听、属地管理、靠前处理"。截至2014年末，12378热线全国转人工呼入总量24.5万个，群众满意度达98.5%。

2014年，全国保险监管机关共接收并处理各类保险消费投诉2.8万件。深入推进保险纠纷调处和"诉调对接"工作，全国保险纠纷调解机构数量达到479个，全年成功调解纠纷案件近2.4万件。与最高人民法院联合推进保险纠纷"诉调对接"机制建设，目前全国已有139个设区的市建立了保险纠纷"诉调对接"机制。

切实解决保险消费者关心的突出问题

一是持续治理"理赔难"。推动财产保险公司优化理赔流程，车险万元以下赔案从客户报案至赔款支付完成的平均时间，由2012年的90.4天缩短至2014年的21.2天。组织开展财产保险积压未决赔案清理，2014年，清理各类财产保险未决赔案734.89万件，清理率为69.62%，涉及

金额950.99亿元。二是深入推进治理"销售误导"。严格落实人身保险客户真实性管理制度，督促公司加大对销售误导行为的责任追究力度。组织开展人身保险失效保单清理专项工作，清理两年以内人身保险失效保单578.03万件，涉及现金价值229.41亿元，清理率达90％以上。三是加大对损害消费者合法权益行为的查处力度。集中力量，针对消费者反映较为集中的保险公司和突出问题开展重点检查。2014年，各保监局共开展涉及消费者权益事项的现场检查4 601次，处罚机构156家，处罚高管人员101人，罚款1 401.3万元，监管谈话348次。

加强与保险消费者有关信息披露

一是全面公布监管政务信息。严格按照政府信息公开要求，通过官方网站全面公布保险监管政策法规、行政许可、行政处罚、工作动态、统计数据等信息。二是定期公布与保险消费者利益相关信息。每季度向社会公布保险公司被投诉数据和被投诉的集中问题，每年通报保险公司消费投诉处理工作考评情况、财产保险积压未决赔案清理情况、人身保险消费者满意度测评情况等。2014年，中国保监会进一步丰富信息披露内容，向社会公布5起损害保险消费者合法权益典型案例。三是及时发布保险消费风险提示。根据保险消费市场不同时期的热点和保险消费者投诉反映的突出问题，采取定期与不定期相结合的方式，通过报刊媒体、互联网络等各种途径，及时发布各类保险消费风险提示，向社会公众揭示保险消费中的风险点、提示保险消费注意事项。2014年，全国保险监管机关共发布各类保险消费风险提示近6 500次。

扎实开展保险消费者教育工作

一是编写出版由项俊波主席作序、梁涛主席助理担任主编的首部保险知识普及读物——《小保学保险》丛书，该丛书被国家新闻出版广电总局纳入农家书屋采购目录。二是拓展保险消费者教育移动平台渠道。开通官方教育微信"保监微课堂"，截至2014年底，仅3个月微信粉丝人数超过7 000人。三是在《中国消费者报》开辟教育专栏，累计刊发稿件31篇，并在中国消费者网同步刊登。四是开展保险公众教育专项活动。在"3·15"国际消费者日和"7·8"全国保险公众宣传日期间，在全国范围组织开展保险宣传教育系列活动，通过刊发宣传稿件，设置宣传展板、宣传栏，发放宣传资料等形式，普及保险知识、宣传保险功能和作用、传播保险历史和文化、倡导科学理性的保险消费理念。

江西保监局建立"四个第三方"推进消费者权益保护工作

江西保监局建立"四个第三方",即建立人身险产品第三方评点制度、建立车险服务质量第三方测评机制、建立保险合同纠纷第三方调处机制和建立保险业参与的第三方鉴定中心,深入推进消费者权益保护工作。

河南保险合同纠纷"诉调对接"工作实现全覆盖

河南各地保险行业协会认真履行保险纠纷调处机制的建设和管理职能,促进保险纠纷调解组织充分发挥作用,通过在法院设立调解室、法院和调解组织合作成立调解中心、成立"保险社会法庭"等形式,实现18个省辖市全面建立保险合同纠纷"诉调对接"机制。2014年,全省保险业通过"诉调对接"机制共调解成功保险合同纠纷1 885件。

保险系统员工摄影作品

08

2015年中国保险市场发展展望

- 行业发展面临良好的外部环境
- 保险行业将取得新的发展成就
- 保险监管工作将迈上新的台阶

行业发展面临良好的外部环境

当前我国经济结构、发展动力、市场机制和面临的国际环境都发生了深刻变化，宏观经济步入新的发展阶段。面对我国经济发展的新常态，党中央、国务院高瞻远瞩，在继续深化改革、简政放权的同时，推动实施了"一带一路"、新型城镇化等一系列创新发展战略。这些战略的实施，有利于推动我国经济结构的转型升级，有利于我国产业结构的调整转型，也为保险业进一步拓宽服务领域、提高服务水平、深度参与社会管理提供了广阔的发展空间。

保险行业将取得新的发展成就

随着保险业发展政策红利的逐步释放，加上党中央、国务院对保险业在国家治理体系和治理能力现代化提出的更高要求，伴随着社会风险意识和保险观念的日益提升，保险行业发展面临良好的市场环境。特别是"新国十条"的出台，标志着发展现代保险服务业已经从行业意愿上升到国家意志。行业定位的重大转变，意味着保险将成为人们的必需品。在我们这样一个保险发展不足的人口和经济大国，未来5—10年将是保险业发展的黄金机遇期。我们有理由相信，2015年保险业仍将实现稳健较快的发展，行业经济效益、社会效益都将得到更好的体现。

保险监管工作将迈上新的台阶

2015年，保险监管将全面贯彻党的十八大、十八届三中、四中全会、中央经济工作会议和习近平总书记系列重要讲话精神，坚持稳中求进工作总基调，主动适应经济发展新常态，深入贯彻保险"新国十条"，持之以恒抓服务、严监管、防风险、促发展，以改革创新为动力，以政策落实为支撑，以防范风险为底线，以保护保险消费者合法权益为出发点和落脚点，促进保险业转型升级和提质增效，努力推动我国由保险大国向保险强国迈进。

保险系统员工摄影作品

保险系统员工摄影作品

09

附录

附录一　2014年中国保险市场重要监管动态

1月8日，中国保监会、中国银监会联合印发《关于进一步规范商业银行代理保险业务销售行为的通知》，自2014年4月1日起实施。该通知从销售对象、产品结构等方面进一步规范银邮代理渠道销售行为。

1月15日，中国保险信息技术管理有限责任公司成立，为保险业发展和监管提供基础性网络支持和信息服务。

1月21日，2014年全国保险监管工作会议在京召开，中国保监会党委书记、主席项俊波出席会议并讲话。

2月19日，中国保监会印发《关于加强和改进保险资金运用比例监管的通知》，整合现行监管比例政策，建立以保险资产分类为基础，多层次、差异化和动态调整的比例监管新体系。

2月21日，中国保监会与美国贸易代表办公室、全美保险监督官协会共同举办的第9次中美保险会谈及中美保险监管研讨会在福州举行。

2月28日，中国保监会印发《关于规范保险资金银行存款业务的通知》，强化交易对手资质审核，建立托管机制，规范存单质押行为，严格信息报告要求。

3月8日，中国保监会办公厅印发《关于做好马来西亚航空飞机失联应急处置工作的紧急通知》，指导保险业做好应急处置和相关善后工作。

3月21日，中国保监会印发《保险公司收购合并管理办法》，适度放宽资金来源和股东资质，允许保险公司同业收购，并规定了强化信息披露、设定收购过渡期、违规行为惩戒等监管措施。

3月25日，中国保监会印发《保险业服务新型城镇化发展的指导意见》，提出六项重点措施，探索保险业服务新型城镇化的体制机制和有效模式，逐步使保险业成为新型城镇化过程中统筹发展多层次城乡保障体系的重要支柱、新型城镇化建设的重要融资渠道、完善社会治理和改进公共服务的重要工具和应对灾害事故风险的重要手段。

4月2日，中国保监会印发《关于授权北京等保监局开展保险资金运用监管试点工作的通知》，授权6个保监局代行部分保险资金运用监管职权，建立多层次的保险资金运用监管体系。

4月24日，中国人民银行、中国银监会、中国证监会、中国保监会、国家外汇管理局联合印发《关于规范金融机构同业业务的通知》，提出同业业务经营、内外部管理、资产负债业务创新等18项要求，助推经济结构调整和转型升级。

5月15日，中国保监会办公厅印发《关于进一步简化行政审批支持中国（上海）自由贸易试验区发展的通知》，推出允许试点航运保险协会条款，取消部分保险分支机构设立及高管任职资格事前审批等三项自贸区内保险监管新举措。

6月6日，中国保监会主席项俊波应邀为西藏自治区党委中心组学习作题为"保险业的改革与发展"的专题授课。2014年，项俊波主席先后赴清华大学以及西藏、浙江、大连、广西等地

进行专题授课，宣讲保险功能作用，推动保险业改革发展。

6月17日，中国保监会印发《关于开展老年人住房反向抵押养老保险试点的指导意见》，鼓励保险业积极参与养老服务业发展，探索完善我国养老保障体系、丰富养老保障方式的新途径。

7月5日，北京保险研究院成立，致力于研究中国保险市场与经济社会前瞻性、战略性问题以及保险监管重大政策制度问题，打造行业智力平台和人才基地。

7月8日，中国保监会举办2014年"7·8全国保险公众宣传日"活动，并向社会发布首份《中国保险业社会责任白皮书》。中国保监会主席项俊波、中国社会科学院副院长李扬出席活动并致辞。

7月17日至18日，第九届亚洲保险监督官论坛（AFIR）在北京举行。论坛选举中国保监会主席项俊波担任新一任轮值主席。

7月28日，中国保监会、浙江省人民政府联合印发《关于在浙江省宁波市建设保险创新综合示范区的通知》，探索可持续、可复制、可推广的保险改革创新之路。

8月10日，国务院印发《关于加快发展现代保险服务业的若干意见》。《若干意见》从经济社会发展战略全局的高度，提升了保险业的行业定位，明确了保险业的战略目标，并从拓宽服务领域、丰富政策体系、深化改革开放等方面对保险业发展进行了系统部署，是未来一个时期中国保险业发展的纲领性文献。

9月4日，中国保险资产管理业协会成立大会暨第一次会员代表大会在北京召开，中国保监会主席项俊波出席会议并讲话。

9月28日，中国保监会印发《保险公司所属非保险子公司管理暂行办法》，采取间接监管模式，加强风险监测，防范风险传递，保护保险消费者利益，促进保险业健康发展。

10月17日，中国保监会印发《关于保险资金投资优先股有关事项的通知》，进一步放开保险资金投资领域，优化资产配置结构，防范保险资金运用风险。

10月17日，中国保监会印发《保险资产风险五级分类指引》，引导保险机构加强全面资产风险管理，提升保险资金使用效率和资产质量。

11月13日，中国保监会发布《保险公司偿付能力监管规则第×号：偿付能力报告（征求意见稿）》，向社会公开征求意见。至此，"偿二代"三个支柱的所有主干技术标准共17项监管规则的征求意见稿已全部对外发布。

11月14日，中国保监会印发《关于加强保险消费者权益保护工作的意见》。《意见》是我国金融监管部门发布的第一个对全行业消费者保护工作作出全面、细化规定的政策性文件。

11月17日，国务院办公厅印发《关于加快发展商业健康保险的若干意见》。《若干意见》是国家第一次从深化医药卫生体制改革、发展健康服务业、促进经济提质增效升级的高度定位商业健康保险的功能作用，也是我国第一个全面部署商业健康保险发展的专项文件。

11月21日，中国农业保险再保险共同体成立大会在北京召开。中国农业保险再保险共同体由23家具有农业保险经营资质的保险公司和1家再保险公司发起组建，致力于整合行业资源，提升农险整体风险管理水平。

12月2日，中国保监会与广西壮族自治区人民政府在南宁签订合作备忘录，就优化保险业发展环境、完善保险市场体系、加大保险资金投资力度等多方面开展深入合作。至此，中国保监会已先后与全国18个省（区、市）和部分计划单列市签订了合作备忘录。

12月4日，中国保监会印发《保险集团并表监管指引》，从全集团角度监测风险，切实防范金融风险传递。

12月12日，中国保监会印发《关于保险资金投资创业投资基金有关事项的通知》，规范保险资金投资创业投资基金行为，支持创业企业和小微企业健康发展，防范投资风险。

12月15日，中国保监会印发《关于开展保险机构"两个加强、两个遏制"专项检查的通知》，通过专项检查摸清保险机构内部管理存在的突出问题和风险隐患，分类处置，并建立防范化解风险的长效机制。

12月18日，中国保监会、香港保险业监理处及澳门金融管理局在澳门签订合作协议，加强反保险欺诈合作。

12月26日，第二次海峡两岸保险监管合作机制会议在北京召开。在既往共识的基础上，双方就进一步深化两岸保险监管合作进行了更加深入、具体的讨论。

12月30日，中国保监会印发《保险机构洗钱和恐怖融资风险评估及客户分类管理指引》，指导保险机构评估洗钱和恐怖融资风险，合理确定客户洗钱风险等级，提升反洗钱和反恐怖融资工作有效性。

保险系统员工摄影作品

附录二   2004–2014年中国主要保险指标

表一   2004–2014年保费及结构①

年份	保费		寿险公司		非寿险公司	
	绝对值（亿元）	增长率（%）	绝对值（亿元）	增长率（%）	绝对值（亿元）	增长率（%）
2004	4 323.0	12.3	3 198.2	7.20	1 124.8	30.0
2005	4 928.4	14.0	3 644.9	14.00	1 283.1	14.1
2006	5 640.2	14.4	4 059.1	11.3	1 581.1	23.2
2007	7 033.4	25.0	4 946.5	21.9	2 086.6	32.0
2008	9 789.1	39.2	7 342.6	48.5	2 446.2	17.3
2009	11 137.3	13.8	8 144.2	11.0	2 992.9	22.4
2010	14 528.0	30.4	10 500.9	28.9	4 026.9	34.6
2011	14 341.0	10.5	9 560.0	6.9	4 780.9	18.7
2012	15 485.5	8.0	9 955.4	4.1	5 530.1	15.7
2013	17 217.9	11.2	10 736.5	7.9	6 481.2	17.2
2014	20 233.6	17.5	12 687.3	18.2	7 546.1	16.4

表二   2004–2014年保险深度、保险密度②

年份	保险深度（%）	保险密度（元/人）
2004	3.39	332.2
2005	2.70	375.6
2006	2.80	431.3
2007	2.93	532.4
2008	3.25	736.7
2009	3.32	834.4
2010	3.65	1 083.4
2011	3.04	1 064.4
2012	2.98	1 143.7
2013	3.03	1 265.4
2014	3.18	1 479.3

表三   2004–2013年保险资金运用收益率

年份	资金运用收益率（%）
2004	2.87
2005	3.60
2006	5.80
2007	12.17
2008	1.91
2009	6.41
2010	4.85
2011	3.57
2012	3.39
2013	5.04
2014③	6.30

① 2004–2010年的保费数据为执行《企业会计准则解释第2号》前的业务口径统计数据。

② 2004–2010年的保险深度、保险密度根据执行《企业会计准则解释第2号》前的业务口径统计数据计算。

③ 2014年GDP为636 463亿元，2014年末总人口为136 782万人，数据来源于国家统计局网站。

表四　2014年各地区保费情况

地区	原保险保费收入			财产保险			人身保险		
	本年累计（亿元）	同比增长（%）	占比（%）	本年累计（亿元）	同比增长（%）	占比（%）	本年累计（亿元）	同比增长（%）	占比（%）
全国合计	20 233.6	17.5	100.0	7 203.5	16.0	100.0	13 030.1	18.4	100.0
一、集团、总公司本级	96.8	13.6	0.5	94.6	13.5	1.3	2.2	6.5	0.0
二、东部地区	11 709.0	17.8	57.9	4 139.6	15.4	57.5	7 569.4	19.2	58.1
北　京	1 207.3	21.3	6.0	314.8	9.3	4.4	892.5	26.2	6.9
天　津	317.7	14.8	1.6	108.9	6.5	1.5	208.9	19.7	1.6
河　北	931.9	11.2	4.6	356.7	15.2	5.0	575.2	8.9	4.4
辽　宁	558	25	2.8	187.4	13.3	2.6	370.6	32.0	2.8
大　连	199.3	13.2	1.0	71.9	13.0	1.0	127.4	13.4	1.0
上　海	986.8	20.1	4.9	320.4	12.3	4.5	666.4	24.3	5.1
江　苏	1 683.8	16.4	8.3	606.3	16.9	8.4	1 077.5	16.2	8.3
浙　江	1 051.1	13.8	5.2	472.9	13.9	6.6	578.2	13.7	4.4
宁　波	207.0	11.6	1.0	111.6	15.2	1.6	95.4	7.6	0.7
福　建	554.7	19.8	2.7	182.2	15.9	2.5	372.5	21.8	2.9
厦　门	131.2	17.4	0.7	57.1	18.6	0.8	74.1	16.5	0.6
山　东	1 250.3	13.5	6.2	426.5	15.1	5.9	823.8	12.7	6.3
青　岛	203.1	13.6	1.0	88.1	17.3	1.2	115.0	10.9	0.9
广　东	1 792.8	25.0	8.9	590.1	21.2	8.2	1 202.7	27.0	9.2
深　圳	548.7	17.1	2.7	207.0	19.8	2.9	341.7	15.5	2.6
海　南	85.1	17.3	0.4	37.8	19.3	0.5	47.3	15.7	0.4
三、中部地区	4 598.9	18.7	22.7	1 460.1	16.5	20.3	3 138.8	19.8	24.1
山　西	465.4	12.9	2.3	156.0	7.9	2.2	309.3	15.5	2.4
吉　林	330.0	25.1	1.6	107.7	18.2	1.5	222.3	28.8	1.7
黑龙江	507.1	31.9	2.5	122.0	7.4	1.7	385.1	42.3	3.0
安　徽	572.5	18.6	2.8	241.4	18.5	3.4	331.0	18.6	2.5
江　西	400.2	25.9	2.0	138.7	19.4	1.9	261.5	29.7	2.0
河　南	1 035.6	13.0	5.1	278.4	16.6	3.9	757.2	11.8	5.8
湖　北	700.1	19.2	3.5	204.6	20.8	2.8	495.5	18.5	3.8
湖　南	588.0	15.7	2.9	211.3	20.0	2.9	376.8	13.4	2.9
四、西部地区	3 828.9	15.4	18.9	1 509.2	17.2	21.0	2 319.7	14.2	17.8
重　庆	407.0	13.7	2.0	138.9	23.4	1.9	268.1	9.2	2.1
四　川	1 060.8	16.0	5.2	371.8	18.0	5.2	689.0	14.9	5.3
贵　州	212.2	16.8	1.1	112.4	26.3	1.6	99.8	7.7	0.8
云　南	376.1	17.3	1.9	177.3	16.8	2.5	198.8	17.7	1.5
西　藏	12.8	11.6	0.1	9.0	13.2	0.1	3.7	7.9	0.0
陕　西	476.9	14.3	2.4	160.0	16.7	2.2	316.9	13.1	2.4
甘　肃	208.4	15.7	1.0	80.0	17.1	1.1	128.4	14.9	1.0
青　海	46.0	17.9	0.2	23.0	17.9	0.3	23.0	18.0	0.2
宁　夏	83.9	15.4	0.4	36.4	15.8	0.5	47.5	15.1	0.4
新　疆	317.4	16.1	1.6	131.6	16.3	1.8	185.8	15.9	1.4
内蒙古	314.0	14.3	1.6	138.3	6.6	1.9	175.8	21.3	1.4
广　西	313.3	13.7	1.6	130.6	16.5	1.8	182.7	11.9	1.4

表五　2014年保险行业资产负债表

资产	年初余额（亿元）	期末余额（亿元）	负债和所有者权益（或股东权益）	年初余额（亿元）	期末余额（亿元）
资产：			负　债：		
货币资金	2 641.0	3 453.4	短期借款	55.5	100.0
拆出资金	0.7	0.7	存入保证金	82.4	546.9
交易性金融资产	1 634.0	2 142.3	拆入资金	25.0	0.0
衍生金融资产	0.3	0.2	交易性金融负债	0.7	100.9
买入返售金融资产	838.2	754.9	衍生金融负债	0.1	0.7
应收利息	1 224.7	1 521.7	卖出回购金融资产款	3 650.5	4 271.4
应收保费	580.0	723.6	应付手续费及佣金	176.5	225.6
应收资产管理费	12.1	18.0	应付营销费用（养老）	0.0	0.0
应收管理费（养老）	3.3	6.6	预收保费	492.7	827.9
应收代位追偿款	41.5	40.8	应付职工薪酬	325.9	466.7
应收分保账款	764.3	681.9	应交税费	139.9	268.2
应收分保未到期责任准备金	393.0	357.7	保险保障基金	29.4	34.3
应收分保未决赔款准备金	562.8	613.4	应付赔付款	951.9	1 149.6
应收分保寿险责任准备金	347.0	1 320.3	其他应付款	487.0	714.7
应收分保长期健康险责任准备金	94.7	103.5	应付保单红利	1 268.2	1 647.8
保户质押贷款	1 335.1	1 800.9	应付分保账款	910.4	1 430.9
贷款	5 526.5	9 297.7	未到期责任准备金	3 325.5	3 793.9
存出保证金	230.0	827.6	未决赔款准备金	3 035.3	3 537.3
定期存款	18 823.0	20 201.0	其中：已发生未报告未决赔款准备金	764.2	993.6
可供出售金融资产	17 889.7	23 120.2	寿险责任准备金	44 428.1	50 501.4
持有至到期投资	21 203.4	22 339.9	长期健康险责任准备金	1 869.9	2 235.7
长期股权投资	3 989.8	6 034.0	保户储金及投资款	9 591.5	12 237.0
存出资本保证金	926.1	1 111.2	长期借款	52.2	20.7
投资性房地产	732.4	824.4	应付债券	2 301.8	2 391.0
固定资产	769.1	811.1	卫星发射保险基金	1.8	1.8
无形资产	272.4	298.7	独立账户负债	823.3	1 096.4
独立账户资产	823.3	1 097.6	递延所得税负债	119.2	399.9
递延所得税资产	212.0	89.2	系统往来（贷项）	54.6	86.9
系统内往来（借项）	61.8	80.3	内部往来（贷项）	65.2	88.2
内部往来（借项）	64.4	85.9	其他负债	186.5	298.4
其他资产	1 042.2	1 805.9	负债合计	74 450.9	88 474.8
			所有者权益（或股东权益）：		
			实收资本(或股本)	3 721.0	4 308.0
			资本公积	2 313.0	4 406.4
			减：库存股	0.0	0.0
			盈余公积	174.1	240.6
			一般风险准备	81.0	514.6
			未分配利润	1 333.1	2 293.6
			外币报表折算差额	−0.8	0.2
			少数股东权益	966.7	1 326.2
			所有者权益合计	8 588.0	13 089.6
资产总计	83 038.9	101 564.4	负债和所有者权益总计	83 038.9	101 564.4